Protect Your Mission

The finance framework
for **nonprofit leaders**

Ryan Alexander

Re think

First published in Great Britain in 2026
by Rethink Press (www.rethinkpress.com)

© Copyright Ryan Alexander

To my extraordinary wife and children,
my greatest source of strength and joy.

And to the nonprofit leaders everywhere who
work tirelessly to make the world better.

Contents

Introduction

As the founder, CEO, executive director, senior executive, or board member of an established nonprofit, there are many reasons why you might have been drawn to this work. You might have a deep desire to tackle difficult challenges and address the inequities you see in the world. Maybe, after a successful professional career, you were ready to lend your financial resources and expertise to a mission that resonated with you. Or you might be an expert in your field (e.g., law, marketing, or operations) hoping your involvement would amplify a nonprofit's impact. This book is written for the leaders responsible for stewarding mission and money, including executive directors, CEOs, COOs, and board members, as well as the philanthropists and foundation staff who fund and oversee this work.

You started down this road because you had a vision for how the world should be. Now you are responsible for a multimillion-dollar operating budget and carry the fiduciary duty to keep your fiscal house in order. Yet, that isn't the reason you are where you are. You want your organization, whether it is a public charity or a private foundation, to solve inequalities, support those in need, champion change-makers, or reinvent how products and services are delivered. These aims are enshrined in your mission. Your mission defines you, and you are proud of it. You know how to deliver impact, and you have been successful at it.

Until now.

Confident as you are in your ability to execute your mission, you have begun to sense that your financial setup is starting to slow you down and create friction that gets in the way of impact. But here's the good news: it doesn't have to stay this way. There is a clear, practical path forward. It might be that you are exiting a relationship with a fiscal sponsor that was managing your back-office functions, and now, almost overnight, you must find a competent, cost-effective solution to a problem you never had before. It might be that your organization has reached a tipping point in terms of growth, and you realize you no longer have the necessary expertise in-house to manage that growth, especially its financial implications.

You recognize the need for a best-in-class finance team, but you don't have the budget to hire the necessary talent or the resources to recruit, vet, and onboard that talent. Perhaps you have tried before and been disappointed by the results. You know you need a finance team that can manage difficult conversations with your auditor and tax accountant and field challenging financial questions from your stakeholders. Those activities are not why you embarked on this journey. They should just ... happen.

Yet somehow, they don't.

After working closely with nonprofits of all sizes, I can tell you that these challenges are fixable. There is a way to keep financial issues from getting in the way of your mission. Whether you are a board member, executive director, or chief operating officer, there is a clear path forward, and this book will show you the way.

I began my career in finance nearly thirty years ago, working grueling hours, building complex financial models, structuring deals, and advising companies on strategic direction. While the work was rigorous and foundational, I wanted more. I didn't just want to analyze businesses from the outside; I wanted to help shape them from within by allocating resources smartly, building strong teams, and implementing systems that drove real results.

That desire led me to executive roles at two software companies, where I gained hands-on experience in scaling operations, aligning strategy with execution, and delivering value to stakeholders. These roles sharpened my perspective on what it takes to build resilient, mission-driven organizations.

Over time, I realized that the same financial rigor that drives businesses forward can transform nonprofits. I shifted my focus to applying everything I learned in finance and industry to organizations creating social impact.

Since then, I have acted as CFO for a wide range of nonprofits, including a large charter school network with a nine-figure budget, a midsize private foundation, a major nonprofit media organization, a youth-serving education organization, and a global organization dedicated to combating youth loneliness and isolation. I have also overseen a series of loan funds totaling $300 million developed in partnership with a prominent American family to help high-performing schools secure long-term facilities, funding the purchase, construction, or renovation of permanent school buildings.

I have worked with top nonprofit auditors, lawyers, and tax accountants, and I have been brought into organizations to oversee the rapid scaling of their operations and impact, as well as to resolve serious accounting challenges. Through this work, I have seen the patterns and problems that even the highest-caliber nonprofits face, and I have learned that with the right structure and support, they are solvable.

At the heart of any successful finance team in a nonprofit are the right personnel and the right technology to execute at a high level, and a solid framework of policies and procedures. I have advised top-performing organizations on financing strategies and ensured that the day-to-day financial reporting tasks are delivered accurately and on time.

These experiences have given me a broad perspective on what works and what doesn't in nonprofit finance: what's needed, what's not, and how to achieve success while avoiding failure. This background has enabled me to create and refine the *IMPACT Framework for Nonprofits*™ to help professionalize your organization's finance and accounting function so you can focus your energy on your mission.

IMPACT stands for:

Internal controls

Management of grants

Planning and budgeting

Accounting and reporting

Cash management

Tax returns and audits

In the chapters that follow, I will walk you through the six components of the *IMPACT Framework for Nonprofits*™, showing you not only what to do, but why it matters, which risks and common missteps to watch out for, and how to bring each element to life in your organization. This isn't a technical manual; it's a practical, field-tested guide to building a finance function that fuels your mission.

To make the IMPACT Framework as practical as possible, each chapter includes a set of tools that are clear, actionable steps you can use to strengthen that specific part of your finance function. These tools are not rigid formulas but practical guides to help you build systems tailored to your organization's size, structure, and needs.

My goal is simple: to help you step out of the weeds, build a finance team you trust, and refocus your energy on what matters most: leading your organization, serving your community, and deepening your impact.

ONE

Problems, Causes, And Consequences

A nonprofit board member called after receiving a three-page management letter from the auditor detailing a litany of financial and internal control deficiencies. "Three pages," I thought. "That's a lot." The auditors warned they would resign unless immediate, drastic changes were made. The CEO and board, believing their house was in order, suddenly realized it was on fire.

The organization had grown to a mid-seven-figure budget, but its finance function had not kept pace. A former administrative staffer had been moved into the finance manager role without the training or systems the job required. This was one of several structural gaps that led to the crisis.

After we implemented changes, the organization kept its auditors, earned a string of clean opinions, and now operates at a high level.

Crises like this are common in midsize nonprofits.

This chapter outlines the most frequent problems, why they arise, and the consequences. These issues apply equally to public charities and private foundations, both of which must understand their own internal systems as well as how their grantees manage funds.

The problems

We'll look first at the problems.

Weak internal controls

Strong internal controls are nonnegotiable: set approval thresholds; govern invoice processing and payments; require independent review of payroll and reconciliations; enforce segregation of duties; leverage appropriate technology; and provide clear channels to report irregularities.

Without adequate internal controls, an organization is vulnerable to errors and internal and external fraud that can be catastrophic, as this example shows.

A nonprofit received a call from someone posing as a regular vendor, claiming to have new bank details. An accounting staffer updated the vendor file and wired a large payment to a fraudster. (Always verify vendor changes with a known contact using a call back to a trusted number.)

Inefficient grants management

The management of grants, particularly restricted grants, is mission-critical. Missteps include overpromising outcomes, chasing off-mission funding, overlapping grant budgets, misallocating restricted expenses, or missing reporting deadlines. Any of these can erode donor confidence and jeopardize future funding. Unlike in the for-profit world, nonprofits must not only spend money wisely but spend it exactly as each donor intended. These restrictions introduce layers of administrative complexity that require precise tracking and coordination across teams.

Flawed planning and budgeting

A disciplined annual budget anchors strategy to spending. Agree on priorities with leaders and department heads, then set responsible spending levels based on size, history, funder mix, and expected grants. Budgeting is also uniquely complicated in nonprofits because much of the revenue is restricted, uncertain, or received on irregular schedules, making accuracy and discipline even more essential.

Once the board approves the budget, operate to it unless the board later approves a revision. Hold budget owners accountable and report budget-to-actuals regularly. If a director spends $15,000 on a conference, was it budgeted and properly approved? If not, another line item may need to be cut to stay on budget.

Every expense should require approval at the right level; larger amounts may require CEO or board sign-off. Without timely reporting and accountability, even a solid budget becomes irrelevant. The point is fiscal stability throughout the year without surprises.

Inaccurate accounting and reporting

The foundation of your organization is accurate GAAP financials, which means recording revenue, expenses, and balance-sheet items correctly; reconciling monthly; and delivering complete, timely financial statements.

When I took over finance and accounting for a private foundation with dozens of investments worth six to eight figures across multiple funds, I discovered a significant tracking error. The foundation had invested in several funds managed by various investment managers. For most managers, each fund investment was properly recorded as a separate line item. However, for one manager, where the foundation had invested in multiple funds, all investments had been incorrectly consolidated into a single entry.

This tracking error caused the foundation to under-report its total assets by more than $1 million. From a reporting standpoint, that money had simply vanished from the books, even though the actual investments still existed.

Insufficient cash management

Healthy liquidity requires deliberate reserves. A pragmatic target is at least six months of operating expenses in reserve (beyond current-year operating cash); one year is ideal but reaching it often takes years. Meanwhile, manage cash flow actively, since pledged or expected funding can be delayed or fall through. Without timely cash forecasts, leadership can't adjust spending when funding is delayed. This challenge is amplified in nonprofits because restricted grants cannot be repurposed for general operating needs, meaning an organization can appear well funded on paper while being cash-poor in practice.

Inadequate audit and tax oversight

Your audit and Form 990 are management's responsibility. Auditors test systems; they don't build them. Address any "significant deficiencies" or "material weaknesses" immediately to preserve funder confidence. Form 990 discloses finances, governance practices, and executive compensation. It's comprehensive and cannot be completed at the last minute.

The causes

Most financial problems stem not from negligence but from growth. As organizations expand, informal systems collapse under the weight of complexity. There are more grants, more staff, and more reporting. Founders who once had a hand in every detail struggle to adapt to the demands of scale.

When the organization was small, the founder could keep tabs on everything informally without documented policies or formal procedures. That approach no longer works once the organization grows into a multimillion-dollar operation. These complexities are part of the growing-up process, but many founders are reluctant to accept or even acknowledge them.

"Financials are just a pain in the ..."

Many leaders feel this way. As discussed in the Introduction, you didn't create or join this organization with the intention of spending all your time on financial matters; you wanted to change the world, and you still do. You would prefer for all this stuff about controls, protocols, and procedures to be somebody else's problem and to have it simply work.

However, once your organization reaches a certain point or size, managing it requires a totally different mindset and skills, perhaps ones you don't necessarily have or even want to acquire. It might be tempting to put your head in the sand and carry on as before, hoping that all will be well.

"Okay, our financials aren't timely, but we're understaffed, and everyone is super busy. These grant agreements are just so complicated nowadays. And, those auditors – wow, what a pain they are! There's always some problem. As for the government, always asking for more, more, more …" Leaders often find themselves thinking along these lines. This complexity reflects a broader trend in philanthropy: major funders increasingly require detailed reporting, measurable outcomes, and compliance with intricate grant conditions. These expectations, while well-intentioned, place heavy administrative burdens on organizations without sophisticated financial systems.

As we will see, hope is not a strategy. By taking a few practical steps, you can avoid the traps that undermine even well-intentioned leaders as their organizations grow.

"My finance team is doing its best"

To have sound financials, you need a high-performing finance team, which is much easier said than done. As I have seen time and again throughout my career, finance professionals often started out doing something else and gradually adapted into a finance role, or they simply never gained the nonprofit accounting and reporting experience required to be strong contributors.

Part of growing as an organization is recruiting the right people to manage its finances. The right job descriptions need to be prepared, interviews conducted, background checks performed, offer letters drafted, and then the team must be managed and directed by somebody intimately familiar with the intricacies of nonprofit finance. All of this takes valuable time when you have a million other things to do.

I cannot stress enough how important it is to have somebody managing the finance team who knows what they need to produce, whether it is generating the myriad of files for your auditor, conducting grant tagging, producing budget-to-actual reports or cash flow analyses for your various stakeholders, or preparing the information for your audit or Form 990 tax filing. In addition, your finance team needs to be able to convey simple, accurate, and actionable concepts to you and your leadership team so that there are no misunderstandings along the way.

One of the essential skills of a good finance person is the ability to talk to different audiences. On the one hand, they might need to have a highly technical conversation with your board treasurer about how to book a particular expenditure or recognize a grant. On the other hand, they need to be able to have a very different conversation with a CEO who may have limited financial knowledge, yet needs clear, digestible insights into whether the organization is going to face a funding shortfall next month, or who wants to be armed with three or four key takeaways to pass on to stakeholders.

"I can't afford financial expertise"

There is an adage: "If you think it's expensive to hire a professional, try hiring an amateur." Yet, countless nonprofits seem to think that many back-office functions, including finance, are not worthy of investment. These functions do not have a visible, immediate impact on how well an organization is achieving its mission, and they are certainly not sexy or exciting.

"We're a mission-based organization, and we need to have impact. Spend the absolute minimum on anything not related to achieving our mission. It's not like it will help us benefit more students, families, or communities." Unfortunately, this is a pervasive attitude among nonprofit organizations. One organization I have worked with has a $12-million operating budget and nearly 100 employees. The organization cut its HR department from five to two people, and that team no longer had a leader. The CFO, to whom the HR department reported, later left. This underscores a pattern among nonprofits that underinvest in back-office resources. Namely, people on those understaffed teams tend to burn out and leave.

Admittedly, while it might make sense for a $25-million-or-more organization to build a robust, multi-person finance department internally, organizations in the $500,000 to $20 million range can acquire the necessary financial expertise far more cost-effectively. You might, for example, pay a specialized company with qualified CFOs and certified public accountants (CPAs) a similar sum as it would cost to hire a mid-level staff accountant. That would be a smart allocation of resources.

The consequences

As we have seen, the consequences of failing to implement proper financial procedures and controls can be nothing short of disastrous. Not only will you have difficulty making rational and effective day-to-day decisions, but you could also run afoul of the law in your state or at the federal level, lose funders you worked so hard to cultivate, have complications with your audit, subject the organization to an increased risk of fraud, and in extreme cases have your organization shut down.

Unreliable decision-making

As a leader or board member, you need to receive the appropriate level of insight into how the organization is performing over a particular period. There are two questions to ask yourself in this regard.

First, does the organization have the necessary levels of cash on hand to continue to fund its operations? For example, while you might be projecting annual receipts of $10 million in grants, if all those funds come in on the last day of your fiscal year, you could have a serious cash flow issue and problems operating the organization.

Second, how is the organization performing against budget? Let's say your organization has a $9-million annual budget, which equates to $750,000 a month on average. If you have spent $4 million in the first three months of the year, there is a real danger that you will run out of funds, unless your organization is highly seasonal or has substantial one-time or capital expenditures.

Having the insight and visibility needed to make timely decisions is critically important. New opportunities and obstacles will inevitably emerge during the year. The organization must be able to decide whether to pursue and invest in those new opportunities and how to deal with those obstacles. It becomes difficult to manage the organization and make decisions without a reliable reference point for performance against budget.

Put simply, a robust budget is the organization's North Star for day-to-day financial management.

Non-compliance

Your organization needs to comply with a wide range of laws, not just one. For example, state and federal laws govern minimum wage requirements and how individuals who perform work for your organization must be classified. Are they performing services as independent contractors or are they deemed full-time employees?

From a finance perspective, the biggest compliance issues revolve around the IRS and federal tax filings required of a nonprofit. Form 990 requires detailed financial reporting along with disclosures about governance, compensation, donor composition, and organizational policies, which is a level of transparency that demands strong systems. Form 990 filing is comprehensive and without solid processes it can quickly become overwhelming. On top of all that, you might need to make state filings, which are often less onerous but nonetheless need to be properly submitted.

If your organization is audited by the IRS or a state-level agency, which becomes increasingly likely as your organization grows, you must be able to produce satisfactory supporting documentation, or you will incur fines and penalties and potentially even lose your tax-exempt status.

In addition to the Form 990 and any applicable state tax filing requirements, your organization may also be required to undergo a financial audit. The requirements vary by state. For example, in New York, nonprofit organizations that register with the Charities Bureau and receive more than $1 million in annual revenue are required to obtain an independent audit conducted by a CPA.

Even if an audit isn't a legal requirement, your funders may insist on one as a condition of continued support. Once your organization reaches a certain size, you might decide to conduct an audit anyway to demonstrate a sound financial structure. If you are looking to raise more money, the lack of an audit could prove a major handicap, as many larger institutional funders require them.

Finally, failing to carry out an audit or receiving a negative audit report will send the wrong signals to board members, funders, and stakeholders, who will wonder whether the organization does, in fact, have its financial house in order.

Negative auditor's report

The goal of every audit is to ensure that your organization receives an unqualified opinion from your auditor. Anything less than an unqualified opinion will require changes and, depending on the scope of the issues identified, could lead to panic among your board members, funders, and stakeholders.

For you, too, it can feel like a sky-is-falling moment. Up to that point, you might have assumed that your finance team was performing its fiduciary responsibilities with a high level of fidelity. Now, suddenly and perhaps without much warning, a major problem has landed in your lap.

Bear in mind that, after spending months combing through the organization's finances, your auditor probably has more insight into the inner workings of the organization than you or your board members. If they have flagged deficiencies, this is your official wake-up call.

If things are so bad that your auditor informs you they no longer wish to work for you (as in the example cited at the start of this chapter), you will need to find a new auditor. This will be challenging because any auditors you approach will want to know why your previous auditor quit.

Shutdown

The worst-case scenario is when an organization's financials are in such dire straits that its tax accountants are unable to prepare accurate tax filings. Such a scenario would undoubtedly lead to investigations from the IRS and state governing authorities, kicking off a process that may ultimately result in the organization losing its tax-exempt status or being shut down.

Introducing the IMPACT Framework for Nonprofits™

The problems outlined in this chapter are all preventable. The following chapters will detail the *IMPACT Framework for Nonprofits*™, which deals with each problem in turn and shows you how to structure your finance function to make your organization robust, resilient, compliant, and successful. In other words, you can ensure that financial failings don't derail your mission.

Summary

- **Lack of experience can lead to crisis:** A financial management crisis can be triggered by a finance individual or team's lack of experience, which can create significant internal control weaknesses and result in your auditor threatening to terminate their relationship with you unless immediate changes are made.

- **Common financial problems must be identified:** Many midsize nonprofits face similar financial issues, such as inadequate internal controls, inefficient grants management, poor budgeting, inaccurate accounting, and insufficient cash management. This can lead to severe operational and reputational damage.

- **Organizational growth can unintentionally create conditions for financial mismanagement:** These problems often arise from the natural growth and increasing complexity of organizations. They can be compounded by a lack of investment in financial expertise and the right people to manage finances as the organization expands.

- **Poor financial management can have severe consequences:** Failing to implement sound financial practices can lead to unreliable decision-making, non-compliance with legal requirements, a qualified or adverse audit opinion, and even the shutdown of the organization due to loss of tax-exempt status or other legal consequences.

- **Problems can be prevented by applying the IMPACT Framework for Nonprofits™:** The *IMPACT Framework for Nonprofits™*, which will be explored in later chapters, offers a process to address and prevent these financial issues, helping nonprofits build robust and resilient financial systems to support their missions.

TWO

Internal Controls

To maintain your organization's integrity and ensure that it can implement its mission, it is critically important to safeguard its assets. For most nonprofits, these assets consist primarily of cash and cash equivalents (short-term, highly liquid investments that can be easily converted into cash), such as money market funds, certificates of deposit (CDs), or short-term government bonds. It is therefore essential that the organization is set up to monitor and protect its cash (and cash equivalents) and to prevent misallocation, whether intentional or unintentional.

To achieve this, a series of checks and balances, or internal controls, must be put in place. Cash controls are a core element of the organization's governance framework, safeguarding resources while influencing related control activities across accounts payable, receivable, and other financial processes.

Internal controls should be applied to all financial processes, including deposits of cash receipts, approval of disbursements, and monthly bank reconciliations for all accounts. These controls should not only specify how the policies should be carried out but also who is responsible for each part of every process, ensuring that all transactions are properly authorized and verified.

Key objectives and requirements

When designing an effective system of internal controls, the goal is always the same: to specify who does what, when, why, and how and to ensure meaningful review and monitoring at every step.

Internal controls have two key objectives: preventing and detecting fraud and ensuring the accuracy of financial records. They should also make it easy to investigate any malfeasance or mistakes that have occurred.

Beyond that, having internal controls in place gives management, the board, and external stakeholders, including donors, confidence that the organization's financial records are true and accurate.

Your internal controls should be enshrined in an accounting policies and procedures manual (sometimes described as a process narrative) that is carefully prepared and endorsed by management and approved by the board of directors. Once finalized, the manual should be reviewed periodically by the board to ensure it reflects current operations and technology.

In addition, it is recommended to have a process map or flowchart that tracks each item in the accounting system from entry to reconciliation. For example, a simple process map for cash receipts might spell out the following. If your organization receives a check as a gift, the system should provide answers to questions like: When should deposits go to the bank? Who should make them? Who should verify them? How should a deposit be entered into the accounting system? Who should verify the entry? How should that transaction be reconciled at the end of the month? How should the supporting documentation be saved, and who should have access to it?

It goes without saying that the individuals responsible for designing internal controls should have complete integrity. It is essential that the board and senior management "set the tone" in terms of the standards required in all the organization's financial operations.

The tone set by senior leadership is critical; everyone else will take their cues from management's attitude toward maintaining strong internal controls.

Equally obviously, the people applying the controls must not only be trustworthy but also be given proper training from internal and external sources. That training should support a mindset of lifelong learning, which is just as important in accounting and finance as in any other professional area.

A system of internal controls need not be complex; indeed, it should be as simple as possible so that it can easily be followed.

Tool 1: Regular monitoring and oversight

The simplest and most effective method of internal control is to regularly monitor the organization's finances. This should be done first through a timely month-end reconciliation process, which will give your internal accounting team the opportunity to discover and investigate any unusual transactions. If your reconciliations are months behind, potential issues will not be identified quickly and can become compounded.

Regular monitoring remains one of the most effective ways to confirm that controls are operating properly and to identify areas needing improvement.

A second effective monitoring tool is an annual budget, prepared by management and approved by the board, which allows the organization to ensure that it is tracking financially according to plan. Once your budget is set, everyone should be on the same page as far as expectations for the year are concerned. Any discrepancies between those expectations and actual results will then be immediately apparent. If, for example, at the end of your second quarter, you have already spent 85% of your budget on a certain line item, you should investigate the reason for this and, if necessary, take action to correct the overspend.

The board also has a role to play in monitoring the organization's finances. Essentially, the board hires the CEO or executive director (who in turn hires management) to implement and execute the organization's mission, which means that the internal controls protecting the organization's assets are also the board's responsibility. In the vast majority of cases, being a board member of a nonprofit is an uncompensated role; board members are involved with the organization because they believe in its mission. For this reason, boards and board members can sometimes deprioritize their responsibilities to the nonprofit as their lives fill with other commitments and claims on their time. That said, it is important for board members to remember that they have a fiduciary responsibility and must constantly keep a finger on the pulse of the organization.

Board oversight is essential. Even with excellent accounting staff, accountability must still flow through regular board-level monitoring.

The final link in the monitoring chain is your auditor. Every time the board engages an external auditor to conduct an audit of the organization, you should expect the auditor to evaluate and gain an understanding of the organization's internal controls. It is a good idea for an organizational leader to have conversations with an auditor before and after an audit to raise any concerns they might have concerning a forthcoming audit and, at the conclusion of an audit, to ask the auditor if they have any concerns, if there are potential weaknesses in the organization's internal controls system, and if the auditor has any recommendations for improving the organization's internal controls.

In general, you shouldn't hesitate to reach out to your auditor as and when issues arise, since they can provide valuable insights and advice. It is certainly preferable to have a discussion with them before a decision is made rather than afterward, in the hope that the decision aligns with the auditor's feedback.

Auditors routinely evaluate internal controls, so consulting with them, especially before making key decisions, can provide invaluable perspective.

Tool 2: Segregation of duties and approval thresholds

As we have seen, internal controls should specify and restrict who is permitted to do what, which means establishing hierarchical approval thresholds for all financial actions. These will obviously depend on the size of the organization and the number and size of its transactions. You might, for example, allow your finance team to approve run-of-the-mill payments of up to $1,000, but require an executive to sign off on amounts up to $5,000, and the CEO or board treasurer to authorize anything above that limit. These approval thresholds are dependent on several factors, including the organization's overall budget, how many payments the organization makes during a typical month, and the average dollar amount of any payment made by the organization.

It is important to think through the appropriate thresholds for your organization to ensure that there is a reasonable degree of trust in those involved in the organization's day-to-day operations and an adequate level of oversight and control over those operations. On the one hand, you cannot have individuals authorizing their own expenses; on the other hand, you do not want senior management to spend all their time signing off on trivial outgoings.

It is also vitally important to ensure that there is a division of responsibilities and segregation of duties in all operations. If the same person is responsible for performing all the steps in a process (e.g., approving invoices and approving the release of payment), it leaves the organization susceptible to the controls being overridden, which could lead to fraudulent activity.

Segregation of duties is critical within your accounting practices. It is recommended that within the accounting team, one person enters the information and another person approves it. In accounts payable, for example, one person should enter the details of a vendor's invoice into the system, another person should approve the invoice, and a third person should release payment for the bill. An environment with multiple checks before an invoice is paid ensures that all the details are correct and the invoice is legitimate. To facilitate this workflow, technology solutions can be adopted to ensure that the rules and required approvals prescribed by the organization's administrator are followed every time for all transactions. Modern accounting and expense systems can also provide audit trails, user-level permissions, and automated approval workflows—critical safeguards when teams are remote or geographically dispersed.

Segregation of duties is essential; no one person should initiate, approve, and reconcile the same transaction.

This is especially important with processes that are repeated, where even a small error can be compounded and cause a potentially catastrophic problem for the organization.

In the case of cash transfers to vendors, they should always be verified with the vendor before the transfer is made to ensure that the amount paid matches the amount invoiced, which should match the vendor's approved quotation, if provided. When an organization is sending funds to a vendor via wire or ACH, the transfer instructions (e.g., bank account number, routing number) should ideally be verbally confirmed prior to initiating the transfer.

You will remember the example in the previous chapter of the phishing scam that cost a client many thousands of dollars. This highlights the importance of using appropriate technology not only to streamline your financial processes and track actions taken within your accounting system but also as an internal control to prevent fraudulent activity. The organization in question had neither an established procedure for checking the identity of a (supposed) vendor nor a technology platform that required the vendor to log in to update their account details. Thus, even though the fraudulent activity was external, it resulted from a weakness in internal controls.

Modern systems can support safe approval workflows and help ensure that payments are only released by the appropriate people.

A related issue is data retention. It is important for organizations to have a clear data retention strategy, covering how long they keep data for, where it is held and in what form, and who has access to it. This involves understanding the legal requirements pertaining to your type of organization. There are typically different requirements for different types of data (e.g., IRS records, state charity registration documents, nonprofits that handle HIPAA-protected records, and personnel files). You should consult an attorney who is well-versed in such matters to determine what is most appropriate for your organization.

Tool 3: Managing conflicts of interest and resource constraints

A common challenge in the context of internal controls is a conflict of interest. It could be, for example, that your organization is looking for a new advertising company and a member of your board happens to run an advertising business, which may give the board member an incentive to promote their company over its competitors. It is imperative for organizations to get into the habit of identifying and managing any potential conflicts of interest. In the above case, it would be necessary for the board member in question to recuse themselves from any decision or even discussion pertaining to the selection of a new advertising company. Organizations should adopt formal conflict of interest policies that are acknowledged in writing annually by all board members, each member of the leadership team, and any other applicable individuals.

In my experience with nonprofits, perhaps the biggest challenge to creating an effective system of internal controls is resources, or, rather, the lack of them. Many organizations are underfunded and understaffed, which means they are reluctant to dedicate resources to, for example, implementing a technology solution that is perceived to merely add to their workload without any tangible benefits for executing their mission.

Faced with a lack of resources, the tendency is to try to save costs on the organization's back office and direct those savings toward programmatic and front-facing activities. As we have seen, however, this can lead to a vicious circle of problems. If there aren't enough accounting personnel to generate timely reconciliations, this will delay the identification of errors or inconsistencies in the organization's financials and compromise their rectification. Worse, the potential for intentional misallocation or misappropriation increases. Either or both of those factors can cost the organization more than it might save by under-resourcing its back office.

There are essentially two methods for overcoming these limitations. First, invest in technology to automate activities and reduce the human element in the process. If your board includes a finance person (who may be the treasurer of the board), they might have a perspective on technology that could improve your financial processes. Similarly, your auditor should be familiar with the latest technology on the market and able to advise you on how it might improve the functioning of your organization.

Second, organizations can outsource various accounting functions. There might seem to be a contradiction between developing internal controls to safeguard your assets and then outsourcing your financial operations to a provider that has a different, independent system of checks and balances, but there can be many benefits to outsourcing.

To begin with, you get access to a best-in-class provider that has experience working for many similar organizations, so it knows what works and what doesn't. In addition, the very fact of engaging an external company means you will avoid having just one person undertaking any process, which provides you with additional control over those processes. Finally, of course, using a third-party provider will prove less costly than hiring full-time staff.

Tool 4: Zero tolerance and whistleblower protections

Having a zero-tolerance policy toward breaches of internal controls is critically important. It may be thought that breaches fall into two separate categories: accidental or unintentional errors due to carelessness or lack of training, and intentional deception. In my experience, however, it is preferable to regard breaches as a continuum, with "mistakes" at one end and "fraud" at the other, since the distinction between them can sometimes be blurred.

To give you an example, I worked with an eight-figure media organization whose accounting and finance team had not done monthly bank reconciliations for nearly a year or downloaded bank statements for six months, yet had continued to issue financials during that time to external stakeholders, funders, management, and the board. At the same time, the organization was processing expense reimbursements without any backup, nobody was approving journal entries entered into its accounting system, and proper documentation was not being furnished for credit card transaction reimbursements. Not only did this run counter to the organization's policies and procedures, but it also showed that it was unlikely that more than one person was reviewing and approving any of the transactions in question.

Another breakdown of the organization's internal controls was the lack of an approval process for journal entries being entered into the accounting system. The organization had very junior accounting personnel entering transactions into the system, and no approver ever flagged the fact that they were incorrect.

Keep in mind that this was the same organization that was issuing financial statements without performing regular month-end reconciliations, yet another breakdown of internal controls.

If your system of internal controls has been carefully constructed, breaches will be rare and, if they do occur, quickly identified. Any breaches of your internal controls should be reported to the appropriate personnel as soon as possible. Depending on the seriousness of the breach, the head of the finance team and/or the organization's leader, as well as the treasurer of the board and/or the entire board, and possibly the relevant authorities, may also need to be notified.

A thorough investigation should take place to gather all the necessary facts to form a clear picture of the situation. The investigation may happen quickly if the breach is a minor error or take months in the case of widespread fraud.

Clear reporting lines are essential; significant issues should always be escalated to the appropriate level of leadership.

If the breach is minor, it may only require additional training for the individual concerned and extra monitoring to ensure that behavior correction has taken effect. Again, this will depend on the scope and impact of the breach. Once a breach has been corrected, it is important to ensure that it doesn't recur by identifying any internal controls that have failed and, if necessary, revising or replacing the relevant controls and updating the accounting policies and procedures manual accordingly.

An important consideration in this regard is the organization's policy on whistleblowing. A well-crafted whistleblowing policy should explicitly encourage employees, vendors, and other stakeholders to report concerns related to financial impropriety, policy violations, or unethical behavior without fear of retaliation. Your accounting policies and procedures manual, as well as your employee handbook, should clearly state the organization's position – that such reporting is welcome and protected.

Best practice includes offering multiple, confidential channels for submitting concerns, such as an anonymous online form, a confidential email address that routes directly to the board or audit committee, and an optional phone line. The policy should also outline how reports are investigated, who is responsible for responding, and the protections in place for whistleblowers. Some organizations use third-party ethics hotlines to reassure staff further that their concerns will be handled discreetly and fairly.

Whistleblowing policies are not just legal protections; they are a powerful internal control mechanism that can catch problems early and foster a culture of transparency and accountability.

Summary

- **Internal controls protect financial integrity:** Safeguarding cash and other assets through robust internal controls is vital to prevent fraud and misallocation. These controls should clearly define responsibilities and verification steps across all financial processes.

- **Monitoring and oversight are crucial:** Regular financial monitoring through reconciliations, budgeting, and board oversight ensures the early detection of issues. External audits also help assess internal control effectiveness and identify areas for improvement.

- **Best practices include segregation and authorization:** Simple but structured processes governing the segregation of duties, hierarchical approval thresholds, and secure vendor verification will reduce the risk of fraud and errors.

- **Resource limitations can be mitigated:** Many nonprofits lack resources, but this limitation can be offset by investing in automation and outsourcing accounting tasks, both of which enhance internal controls without overburdening staff.

- **Zero tolerance and reporting culture matter:** Breaches must be treated seriously, investigated promptly, and reported according to severity. A culture of transparency and whistleblower support helps maintain accountability and reinforces control systems.

THREE

Management Of Grants

As a nonprofit, your organization most likely generates the bulk of its revenue from grants and donations. Those grants typically come with specific requirements related to how and when funds can be used, what results must be delivered, and what reporting is expected. Managing those obligations well is essential to sustaining your revenue and the programs that depend on it. When grants are mishandled, funders may withdraw their support, and in the nonprofit sector, word travels fast when an organization is seen as "not to be trusted" with donor dollars.

In preparing this chapter, I spoke with Ana Morgado, Controller at Civic News Company and a former nonprofit auditor with more than twenty years of experience in nonprofit finance. She was quick to emphasize the vital importance of good grants management for this reason.

"Once you lose the confidence of your funders, it's tough to get it back."
Ana Morgado, Controller,
Civic News Company

What is often overlooked is that grants management is fundamentally a collaborative process. It requires coordination between the organization and the funder, between the development team and the finance team, and the active involvement of leadership to ensure that the objectives of each grant are implemented with fidelity.

Tool 1: Prepare mission-aligned, realistic grant requests

The grants management process typically begins with a proposal drafted by your organization and submitted to a potential funder, such as a private foundation, corporate funder, or high-net-worth individual. Occasionally, a funder may simply say, "I love the work that your organization is doing, here's a check, and you can spend it however you want." But those unrestricted gifts are typically the exception. In most cases, you will need to submit a formal request that outlines the program you want to fund and includes a detailed budget tied to the amount you are requesting.

If the funder agrees to move forward, they will issue either a grant agreement or an award letter. These documents will specify the funding amount, the payment schedule, and how the funds must be used. In other words, they come with restrictions and conditions.

This is why it is so important to be thoughtful and precise about how you describe your program and what your organization commits to delivering in the grant proposal. For example, if you write, "We plan to serve 500 youth," you shouldn't be surprised when the agreement requires you to serve exactly 500 youth within a defined timeframe. What you propose is what you are expected to deliver, often to the letter.

There are additional factors to keep in mind when drafting grant proposals. First, your development and finance teams must be tightly coordinated. For example, a single program cannot be fully funded multiple times by different donors. If you have a program with a $1-million budget and end up securing $3 million in restricted funds earmarked for that program, your organization may be required to return the excess. In worst-case scenarios, this can damage donor trust and harm your reputation. One strategy is to use a live 'sources-and-uses' tracker by program to prevent accepting restricted dollars that exceed an approved program budget.

Second, while it is tempting to pursue funding tied to trending issues or "hot topics," you must ensure that every grant request aligns with your organization's core strategy. Taking on programs outside of your mission merely to chase funding can lead to mission drift, staff misalignment, and long-term financial strain.

"Many donors are eager to fund programs addressing the latest social crises. In turn, organizations often create initiatives or programs that try to bridge those emerging issues with their existing mission. Sometimes that alignment works, but often it doesn't. It's essential to stay true to your mission and to the community you're meant to serve."
Ana Morgado

Funders will often gravitate toward "sexy" projects and may be less interested in funding the underlying work that you do or your organization's day-to-day operations. Your funders may offer you a restricted grant for Program Y because it is shiny and new, but you still need to make payroll and pay your bills to keep the lights on. This is where things can get tricky, and you may need to have a conversation with a funder to try to persuade them to move those funds into a different project or program that will help you to cover your day-to-day operating costs or designate those funds for general support. Any change in purpose or timing should be confirmed in writing, signed by both parties, before you reallocate or spend.

Third, you should consider what you will do if your potential funder doesn't fund the whole cost of the program. If, for example, you say that the budget for Program X is $500,000 and the funder decides to provide only half or a certain percentage of that sum on the condition that you obtain the rest from other donors, you will need a concrete plan to raise the remainder so you can deliver the outcomes you've committed to.

Tool 2: Honor grant restrictions, conditions, and cash flow realities

A grant award can be restricted by time or purpose, or both. It may stipulate a period during which or a date by which the funds must be spent. It may specify exactly what the funds are to be spent on, for example, "helping youth in Los Angeles," which would mean that you couldn't use that grant to help youth in Phoenix or Delaware.

The award will likely also specify when the funds are to be paid: either in a single payment or, more typically, in installments. In the latter case, those payments might be conditional on the organization achieving, and evidencing that it has achieved, certain quantifiable goals or "milestones" pertaining to the funded program (e.g., you must have served a certain number of students or those students must have achieved certain outcomes). As mentioned in the previous section, these goals will often be based on the proposal that you originally submitted to the funder.

"Once you satisfy the conditions or hit the milestones, you must usually submit an interim report to the funder. They'll review the outcomes, and, if they're satisfied that the milestones have been achieved, they'll give the organization the next tranche of funding that's due."
Ana Morgado

This means that if you miss a program deadline or submit an inadequate or incomplete report, you risk not receiving subsequent tranches of funding from that funder and ultimately jeopardizing your program. (We will discuss the importance of timely and accurate reporting in Chapter 5.)

If the award is a cost reimbursement grant, which is common for state or federal funding initiatives, you will need to submit proof of the relevant expenses having been incurred before the funds are disbursed. It is important to keep in mind the potential cash flow implications for your organization of these types of grants, since expenses must be incurred before they are eligible for reimbursement by the funder. Build a working-capital plan (e.g., internal reserves or a board-approved line of credit) so you can cover expenses before reimbursement arrives.

From an accounting perspective, recognize conditional grants as revenue only after the conditions are met; until then, record them as a refundable advance (liability). Recognize unconditional grants upon receipt; if restricted by time or purpose, record them in net assets with donor restrictions until satisfied. A condition exists when there's both (i) a measurable barrier (e.g., specific outcomes, approved reports) and (ii) a right of return or release if not met—even if the gift is otherwise unrestricted. If a program will not proceed or conditions won't be met, be prepared to return the funds.

"If you spend the funds but don't meet the grant's conditions or can't provide documentation showing that the money was used as agreed, the funder may feel that their gift was used for something they didn't intend or approve."
Ana Morgado

Tool 3: Build a precise tagging and tracking system

Collaboration between the development and finance teams is important because, ultimately, finance is responsible for ensuring that expenses are properly tagged to a particular grant.

"You should have a clear, consistent system for making sure the eligible expenses are charged to a specific grant and align with that grant's intended purpose."
Ana Morgado

It is essential to avoid double-dipping (i.e., allocating the same expense to more than one grant). If your organization requires an audit (see Chapter 7), this is something your auditor will prioritize testing for, as any such misrepresentation of how the organization is spending a funder's money can have serious consequences.

Tagging general operating costs to the appropriate funds is no simple matter. In fact, it can be a puzzle, to say the least. Essentially, you need to ensure that the expenses you tag to a particular funder align with whatever you have committed to that funder while also ensuring that other expenses that remain untagged will be sufficient to satisfy the requirements of your other restricted grants. A single expense (e.g., rent or an individual employee's salary) can also be allocated to multiple grants. In such a scenario, the CEO of the organization, for example, may be tagged to six different grants based on how they spend their time and the objectives of each grant.

It is crucial to stay on top of the grant tagging process, not only to satisfy the conditions and requirements of your existing funders, but also so that your development team knows at any given time what they can and cannot request of new funders. If, for example, you have Funders A through F giving you different grant amounts for different programs across different time periods, and your development team is approaching Funder G for another grant, the development team must not be allowed to "promise" Funder G that their gift will be put toward expenses already covered by grants from Funders A to F. If your records are not accurate and up to date, it becomes difficult for the development team to know what to tell Funder G. You also run the risk of double-dipping, as discussed above.

Accurate and timely tagging, along with close coordination between finance and development, becomes increasingly vital as your organization grows and attracts more funders.

If you are a small organization with only a few funders, quarterly tagging might be sufficient. But what if a grant report is due before the end of a quarterly period? Your report will not be up to date and will be incomplete or inaccurate. Tagging should therefore be done at least monthly and performed as part of the monthly reconciliation process.

"A small organization might get away with charging grant expenses only at the end of each quarter, every

six months, or when funder reports are due. Ideally,
however, you should plan expenses in advance so
that as soon as they're incurred, you can immediately
charge them to the appropriate grant."
Ana Morgado

Solving the tagging puzzle is largely a question of staying organized, having a process in place, and ensuring that everyone understands who is doing what (particularly in terms of the interplay between finance and development), what the reporting requirements are (see Chapter 7), and when the deadlines need to be met.

There isn't one right way to do all this, but it does require commitment to the process and the allocation of sufficient time and effort to ensure it is done properly. Inevitably, as the sophistication and complexity of your organization increase, so too must those of your grants management processes. Where initially a spreadsheet or QuickBooks sufficed, you might eventually need to incorporate specialized grant management or donor tracking software into your organization's technology ecosystem.

However you do it, the first thing your auditor will want to see is that your organization has some mechanism for keeping track of expenses related to grants, and you can be sure that they will test it. They will look at the proposal and the budget submitted by the organization to the funder. They will request supporting evidence, including emails and other communications, as well as your regular reports to the funder. Finally, they will check that everything matches and that the donor's money is being spent according to how your organization has committed to spending it. If it doesn't, you will have a problem.

"If your organization manages multiple grants, you need an accounting structure robust enough to track and keep everything organized. This helps ensure you don't double-dip, charging the same expense to more than one grant, or run out of eligible funds to charge to specific programs."
Ana Morgado

Keep in mind that your auditor will assess your organization's compliance with the grants you have received, including the associated terms, which often align with your funders' expectations. If your organization receives city, state, or federal grants, the audit will be even more rigorous, as auditors must follow strict government guidelines.

Tool 4: Create a shared compliance and reporting calendar

As we have discussed, funders want to see evidence not only of how their funds are being spent, but also of the impact those funds have. Funders will therefore insist on regular progress reports, typically every six months or annually. The more sophisticated the funder, the greater the reporting demands they are likely to make. It is essential to know and adhere to the required reporting deadlines for each grant. One way to successfully manage many grants and various reporting deadlines is to maintain a single compliance calendar (owner, due date, status) shared by development, programs, and finance.

It is not enough to provide your funders with a qualitative narrative describing the work that has been done against the program that is being funded; they will demand quantitative statistics on the relevant financials and outcomes. They may insist that you report metrics around how many homeless people were served and how many facilities were opened, for example, which may be specified in the grant award.

We will look at reporting in more detail in Chapter 5, but it is worth noting here that progress reports sent to your funders should be taken seriously. It is important for those reports to be prepared in a professional manner and be comprehensive and highly accurate, because you are in a formal contractual business relationship with the funder, and you want to ensure that you aren't giving that funder any excuse not to continue funding your organization.

Tool 5: Treat funders as partners through proactive communication

Progress reports aren't the only kind of communication funders might require. If a funder is supporting a local organization because it is within its community and they want to have (and be seen to have) a positive impact on the community, they might want to know what is happening with the program far more frequently than every six months or once a year. If the grant is large enough, the funder may even want to appoint somebody to the organization's board.

Whatever their demands, being completely transparent and maintaining an open line of dialogue with your funders is essential. It is not just a business relationship but a partnership. The funder is (or should be) excited about funding the work that your organization is doing.

Should the focus of the organization or a particular program change in any way during the term of a grant, you must have a conversation with your funders. Keeping funders updated on the latest developments ensures that there are no surprises when they receive your progress report and discover that your spending differs from what they anticipated.

"If your donor gives you funding to help the elderly, you certainly don't want to have to say

> *to them, 'We know your gift was meant to help*
> *the elderly, but we had a shortfall in our youth*
> *program, so we used the funds there instead.'"*
> Ana Morgado

Conversely (and another reason why you should be in regular communication with your funders), you will want to know as soon as possible if your funders are considering changing their programmatic investment focus so that you aren't caught off guard if they suddenly announce that they are terminating their funding to your organization. Ultimately, you must not lose sight of the fact that funders are the ones with the money and decide what they do with that money. Programs that funders supported last year or the year before might not be their priority in the coming year. Regular communication with your funders should help you to manage these dynamics as well as possible.

Tool 6: Resolve grant issues early and prevent repeat problems

As we have seen, funders want to support your mission and vision and be confident that your organization has the appropriate policies and procedures in place to act as good stewards of their gift. Any carelessness around meeting funders' reporting requirements can dent that confidence and damage your relationship with funders. Apart from not being timely with your report submissions, examples of such carelessness include submitting reports that have not been proof-read or reports in which the budgets do not match what the grant agreement with the funder detailed.

Another area where organizations get into trouble is not spending restricted dollars according to what was agreed between the funder and the organization, or not spending funds at all because the organization has raised too many restricted dollars for a particular program or initiative, and it simply doesn't have any other costs that can be tagged to that grant. This can necessitate going back to the funder and saying, "Sorry, we haven't spent your dollars yet. Instead of funding Program A, would you be interested in Program B? Or would you like us to refund the unspent portion of your grant?"

Most funders are mission-aligned and will work with organizations to reassign or extend grant terms rather than request repayment. However, repayment is always an option they reserve and a risk to your organization, particularly if the relationship with the funder has deteriorated. In most cases, though, you can engage the funder to extend the grant period or reallocate the funds to another project aligned with their intent.

"Most funders won't say, 'Oh, you didn't spend the money? Too bad, give it back.' If a grantor has supported your organization, it's usually because

> *they believe in your mission and feel connected to the work you're doing. In many cases, they'll be open to working with you to reassign the funds to another purpose or to extend the grant period."*
> Ana Morgado

All of that said, it is far better not to put your funders and yourself in that position to begin with.

As we have discussed, grants may be categorized as restricted or unrestricted and as conditional or unconditional. Each of these designations carries slightly different accounting implications:

- Restricted funds must be tracked carefully and only spent on the purposes outlined by the funder.

- Conditional grants may require specific deliverables, such as serving a certain number of clients or submitting approved reports, before funds are released or recognized.

- Unrestricted and unconditional grants, in contrast, can generally be recognized and spent at the organization's discretion.

These distinctions are not just technicalities; they affect your organization's cash flow projections, reporting, and, ultimately, your funders' trust in your financial stewardship.

We have also seen the vital importance of coordination between finance and development to avoid development securing more funds for a program or initiative than it will cost.

All these potential problems lead us back to the need for effective internal controls discussed in Chapter 2.

Tool 7: Right-size your development and grants capacity

Typically, the larger the organization's operating budget, the more sophisticated its development approach should be. At the smaller end of the range, organizations can rely on the executive director to submit proposals and reports. At the larger end, there will be an entire department with various teams within it focused on different sizes of donors, donors in different geographic areas, transformational gifts, donors who are only interested in funding certain types of programs, and so on. In between, there are organizations that may rely on an external consultant to help manage their grants.

Within a nascent or smaller nonprofit, incorporating a consultant into its development ecosystem could be preferable to bringing in a full-time employee, given the associated costs and management responsibilities. By outsourcing, you will also be able to leverage somebody with deep domain expertise. If you decide to use a third party for development and grants management, however, it is more important than ever to ensure that there is close consultation with finance so that everything is properly aligned.

Whichever path you follow, keep in mind that there must always be a return on your investment in development. Unlike nearly every other role in the organization, your development manager or team should be generating revenue. As a planning benchmark, many organizations target contributed revenue of ~3–5x fully loaded compensation for dedicated development roles calibrated by donor mix, gift pipeline maturity, and the ramp time for new staff.

Your development strategy may rely on a consultant, a full-time employee, or a mix of both. The key is to determine which option is most likely to drive your organization's success.

Tool 8: Apply strong grants management when you are the funder

As a private foundation, your priority will be to create an infrastructure that helps to ensure that the funds you disburse to grantees are used in accordance with your foundation's overall mission and goals. There are two primary strategies here. One is a restricted or project support grant by which you use the terms of your grant agreement with a grantee to dictate how the funds your foundation disburses are to be used and the metrics the foundation wants the grantee to achieve during the term of the grant. This is a common approach that establishes clear objectives and expected outcomes agreed to by the foundation and the grantee prior to the disbursement of funds.

The other approach is not to restrict the funds disbursed to a grantee (an unrestricted or general support grant). In this approach, it is important to note that you, as the foundation, theoretically lose control over how the grantee spends those funds. I say in theory because, if a grantee doesn't use the funds in a manner consistent with the foundation's mission, the foundation can always opt to stop funding the grantee in the future. This second option tends to promote a partnership arrangement between the foundation and the grantee. Generally, awarding unrestricted gifts is the approach used by foundations where there is a level of trust and a longer history with a grantee that gives them confidence that the funds will be used in a manner aligned with the foundation's mission and goals.

In either scenario (a restricted or unrestricted grant), the foundation will most likely request periodic progress reports from a grantee to track the grant's impact on the community being served.

Foundations should always do their due diligence on prospective grantees, as well as on those grantees they continue to support. Read through a grantee's audits for the past couple of years. Review the grantee's latest Form 990 tax filing, which can be easily accessed online. Ask the grantee for any management letters they have received from their auditor, which may provide you with insights into any internal control deficiencies at the organization. Finally, speak regularly with the grantee's management and board members to ensure that you have your finger on the pulse of the latest developments at the organization.

"If you're the one making the grant, you'll want to be sure the organization you're funding has sound accounting practices and internal controls in place to ensure your money truly benefits the population you intend to serve."
Ana Morgado

Summary

- **Grants management is crucial:** Proper grants management is essential to maintaining donor trust and sustaining revenue. Mismanagement can damage reputations and lead to loss of funding in a closely connected nonprofit sector.

- **Cross-team collaboration is vital:** Effective grants management requires coordinated efforts between development, finance, and leadership teams. Misaligned or overfunded programs can result in having to return funds or breaching donor agreements.

- **Compliance and reporting are non-negotiable:** Grants often come with strict usage, timing, and reporting conditions that must be met. Inadequate tracking, incomplete reports, or missed deadlines can jeopardize funding and future donor relationships.

- **Accurate tagging and accounting matter:** Each grant-related expense must be tagged correctly and aligned with donor restrictions to avoid double-dipping. Regular tagging, monthly reconciliation, and up-to-date records are essential for accountability and audit readiness.

- **Proactive communication prevents issues:** Maintaining open and transparent communication with funders helps manage changes, avoid surprises, and resolve problems. Whether in-house or outsourced, development efforts must be strategic, financially justifiable, and closely linked with finance.

FOUR
Planning And Budgeting

A ccurate planning and budgeting are essential to achieving your organization's goals and ensuring that its financial resources are aligned with its mission and objectives. In simple terms, your aim is to achieve the maximum output with the resources you have.

I also spoke with Charlie Haraway, Founder and Chief Executive Officer of Millennia Park, regarding planning and budgeting.

Tool 1: Set your North Star and design the plan backward

It is essential for an organization to set a North Star for its work. This means aligning as many aspects of the organization's work and its investments as possible with its mission. This serves two purposes. First, it focuses your discussions and decisions. For example, if preserving and protecting native wildlife habitats is the cornerstone of your organization, it would be detrimental to have a board member who believes that you should also expand public access to affordable housing by developing that same land. You must ensure that there is alignment with the organization's mission, because that will dictate not only the work that is done (and not done), but also the types of people you need to hire and engage to do it.

Second, it will prevent your organization from being tempted to accept funds from just any donor willing to write you a check. Funder Z may be particularly interested in supporting a new initiative or endeavor, but is it sufficiently aligned with your organization's North Star to make those funds acceptable?

Accepting funding for a new initiative almost always requires hiring staff to run it. In the event the funder loses interest in the work and you are unable to continue to fund the program a year or several years after you receive the initial funding, you could be in a situation where you need to terminate the individuals you hired to implement the program. This can result in distraction and disruption within the organization for a program you may not really have wanted to undertake in the first place.

Identify your core mission, then evaluate any new initiatives in relation to it. The core programs of your organization should ideally represent the bulk of your budget.

You must also have an idea of where you want your organization to be financially at the end of the year. Do you want to break even? Do you want to raise enough funds to create new programs in the future? Do you need to focus on raising a reserve fund for a rainy day?

"To make it actionable, your plan must be backward designed."
Charlie Haraway, Founder and Chief Executive Officer, Millennia Park

---

In practice, this means starting with outcomes and building the numbers to match, not the other way around. Many organizations simply take last year's budget and increase it by a percentage, but incremental budgeting without a clear purpose misses the point. Effective plans are built backward from mission and goals, not forward from last year's numbers.

As you start to prepare the next fiscal year's operating budget, begin early and work backward from mission-aligned goals. The complexity, size, and clarity of your organization's mission will determine how long the process takes. Organizations with clear, focused missions move quickly; those still refining their mission typically need a longer, more iterative process.

As a rule of thumb, most nonprofits should begin budgeting three to six months before year-end; large or multi-entity organizations often benefit from nine to twelve months of rolling planning. However far ahead you plan, you should incorporate contingency planning into your budgeting work. These contingency plans will require intentional and meaningful conversations with the appropriate stakeholders. It cannot just be the CEO or executive director who decides what to do when something doesn't go according to plan.

Another key aspect of the planning and budgeting process is conservatism, which has different implications for revenues and expenses. On the revenue side, it is key not to make overly aggressive assumptions about fundraising and any earned revenue the organization anticipates generating. You may have fifty prospective funders in your pipeline, but it would be reckless to assume they will all close for the amounts they indicated they might be interested in funding. Be realistic, or even a little (or very) pessimistic, when it comes to budgeting likely revenues.

In terms of expenses, it means not underestimating the cost of running your organization. This requires a comprehensive review of all the organization's cash outflows, including all personnel costs – not only their rates of pay but also travel expenses and benefits, as applicable. It also means factoring in some buffer so that, if something unexpected that makes sense to invest in comes up, the organization can accommodate it. Keep in mind, too, that inflation can significantly impact organizations' budgets and should be factored into your assumptions.

Regarding technology to leverage the budgeting process, for most smaller organizations, Excel or Google Sheets are perfectly adequate budgeting tools. As organizational complexity, size, entity count, or country footprint increase, you will likely need to adopt more sophisticated budgeting and accounting platforms, but any such upscaling should be carefully considered in advance.

Tool 2: Build genuine stakeholder buy-in

When planning and budgeting, it is important to ensure that you have buy-in from key stakeholders to align resources with the mission. Depending on the specifics of the organization, stakeholders can include the management and leadership of the organization, the board (or a committee, like a finance committee, designated by the board), prospective and current funders, and even the wider community in certain instances. As a leader, you must synthesize the feedback you receive to ensure that investments are made where the organization can have the greatest near-term and long-term impact.

While financial strategy and priorities are often determined by the senior leadership team and/or the CEO or executive director and approved by the board, the implementation of the budget is done at a much more granular level by managers and department heads. So, it is important to ensure buy-in from those team members as well, because they ultimately do a large portion of the day-to-day work. Avoid a top-down handoff ("Here's your budget. Stay within it."). Rather, build a back-and-forth with senior managers to understand how they'll achieve their part of the mission.

Being collaborative and transparent doesn't mean giving your managers the impression that you have an endless checkbook and that, from a budgeting point of view, the sky is the limit. You must make them aware of the realities of funding limitations. At the same time, you should listen to them to understand their budget issues and learn from them how best to allocate the budget or make the most successful investments of available funds. I have often found these exchanges to be an illuminating and valuable piece of the budgeting process.

Boards, too, expect transparency. They have a legal and ethical fiduciary responsibility to the organization and expect to have a level of ownership and collaboration with management during the budgeting process. As we have discussed, presenting a budget to the board as a *fait accompli* is not the best strategy. Instead, there should be a series of meetings and a two-way discussion with board members. Rather than simply stating during a board meeting without any prior context, "We are now asking the board to vote to approve the budget for the upcoming year," you will be saying, "As we have discussed with you during the past several weeks and based on your feedback, we believe that we are making the right investments next year for X, Y, Z reasons. We, therefore, would like the board to approve the budget for the upcoming year."

In practice, that means previewing major assumptions with the finance committee, socializing deltas early, and arriving at the vote with no surprises. It is helpful for the board to understand the decision-making process that the leadership team followed to reach the conclusions they did. Failing to appropriately involve the board in the budgeting process can backfire in more ways than you can imagine. Just when you believe you are ready for the board to vote to approve the budget, a board member will raise a question regarding the proposed budget that management hasn't thought about, causing a problem that could have been avoided.

There are limits to collaboration: boards set guardrails, but staff closest to the work should draft the first budget and own the operational plan.

It is important not to overlook the needs of the community you serve as you go through the budgeting process. Your leadership team should be in the field periodically to really understand programmatically what is and is not working well, what needs to be changed, and why.

Having an ear to the ground in this way will enable you to respond more effectively to changing circumstances and to bring your funders along with you. If a program is not receiving as positive a reaction from the community as it once did and you sense that a shift in focus or even a change of tack is required, you will be well-equipped to persuade your funders that a revised strategy is necessary to deliver better results to the community you are serving.

Finally, during the year, events will arise that impact the budget in ways you didn't anticipate when it was established and approved by the board. To prevent surprises at the board level, it is important for you to be transparent and in touch with the board, letting them know what is happening in the field and how that might be impacting the number of new hires, for example. Alternatively, you may have funding fall through. In that case, you should present to the board your plan for raising additional funds and/or cutting costs, and why you are proposing to reduce the costs you are. The board may disagree with you, but at least they will be aware of the reasons behind the recommendations.

Tool 3: Allocate resources using your North Star

When it comes to allocating your scarce financial resources across various programs within your organization, you should always come back to your North Star. The first part of the budgeting process should be ensuring alignment with the organization's mission, because that informs where funds are allocated.

If we visualize your mission, your funder universe, and the target market you serve as three circles, they would ideally line up exactly one on top of another. In reality, they will never overlap completely. You will inevitably have funders who press you ("It'd be really great if you could start doing this.") or change their minds ("I'm not so excited about that program anymore, but I'm willing to invest in this."). As much as you want to and try to, you will most likely never serve every member of your target community. Nevertheless, your job is to create as much overlap between the three circles as possible, to ensure that you are addressing the needs of the community you serve (target market), the intentions of the funders who are providing financial resources to your organization, and your organization's overall mission.

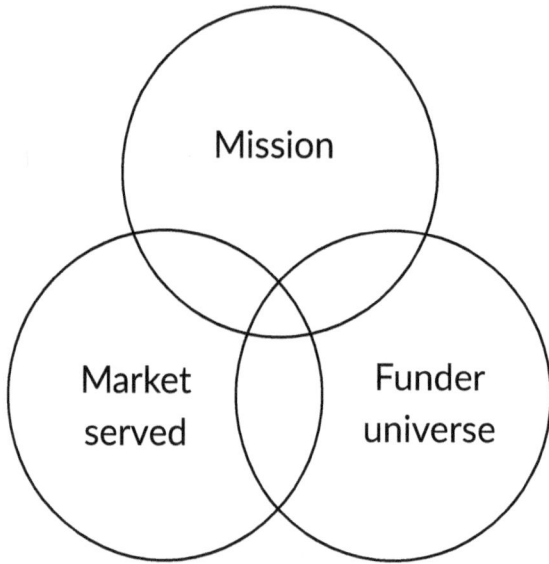

Mission

Market served

Funder universe

Staying close to stakeholder feedback is essential to navigating these discussions effectively. The same applies to resource allocation decisions. Organizations need to be mindful of the feedback they receive from the market regarding the work they are doing. Markets change and shift, and adjustments may need to be made. If, for example, your organization wants to have an impact on youth in a particular way but is increasingly having difficulty attracting funds for that program, you may need to adjust your focus so that you are still serving the same population but in a different or more efficient way.

Any reallocation of resources, however, must be in line with the organization's mission and values. These adjustments might therefore dictate that you need to cut back on team-building events or cancel this year's gala, but keep staff hired or retain the program manager so that your operations can continue.

To put it another way, the organization needs to focus its resources to maximize the likelihood of achieving the outcomes it has promised to funders and the community.

Tool 4: Build and use your reserve fund wisely

Once resources are allocated, the next step is ensuring long-term financial stability through thoughtful cash management. Many nonprofits approach the budgeting process as a breakeven exercise, with all the funds raised during a budget year projected to be spent. Increasingly, however, nonprofits are budgeting to generate excess funds by the end of the budget year to ensure the long-term sustainability of the organization.

A major catalyst for this change in thinking was the COVID-19 pandemic, which challenged the staying power of many nonprofits (and other businesses) as funding streams were suddenly impacted.

Organizations that did not have adequate reserves to weather a modest degree of business interruption were forced to reduce staff and scale back programmatic initiatives. Other organizations were forced to wind down amid the funding chaos created by the pandemic.

Another challenge that organizations regularly face is that market changes typically do not align with their budget year, and they may need to adjust their programs mid-year. If, during the year, you determine that Program A is not working, you might decide to wind it down and, if the funds are unrestricted or the funder agrees to a revised use, reallocate those funds to a new program. These changes can take time to implement as one program is phased out and a new program is phased in. Having a reserve fund can help navigate the shift and ensure that your organization maintains positive momentum throughout the transition.

Your fundraising team is always looking to raise money for future years, which is an uncertain business. When you are budgeting for the coming year (assuming your entire budget has not already been raised with the cash in the bank), you will need to estimate whether certain funders will come in and, if so, for how much. In doing so, you should base your current year's budget not only on the predictability of the funder, but also on that of the funders in general and the economy overall.

Another approach to mitigating the lack of a reserve fund is to base your coming year's budget on funds that have been raised and are in the bank ahead of the start of the year. This removes a lot of the guess-work and angst around funder expectations and provides you with a year to raise the budget for the following year. For example, if you are projected to enter 2027 with $8.3 million of cash in the bank, your 2027 budget should not exceed $8.3 million. You then have 2027 to raise the cash for your 2028 budget. If, based on funds raised during 2027, you will enter 2028 with $7.6 million, your 2028 budget should not exceed $7.6 million.

That said, establishing a reserve fund will provide you with the ultimate buffer against uncertainty. In the event, for example, that you project that fund-ing from a particular funder will materialize during your current budget year, but that funding doesn't come through, a healthy reserve fund enables you to continue funding the relevant program, should that be in your long-term interest. While you may decide that you and your board don't want to tap into your reserve fund, you at least have that option to maintain continuity of operations.

As difficult as it may be, it is crucial for organiza-tions to work to establish a rainy-day or reserve fund: cash that is set aside and unrestricted, allowing the organization to do whatever it needs to do. This, of course, is easy to say, and it is every organization's dream to have multiple years of funding in the bank, but often the reality is quite different. Setting aside reserve funds requires considerable discipline and determination.

You must decide how much you need to set aside for a reserve. Optimally, a reserve fund should cover three to six months of operating expenses, with twelve months being a strong ideal depending on the organization's funding volatility.

Keep in mind also that, as your reserve fund begins to grow, you may be questioned, "Why have you got so much cash? You're a nonprofit, why are you holding on to all that money?" While such questions from prospective or current funders may seem justified, it is important that nonprofits convey a position of financial sustainability and responsibility and can justify their reserves through their impact reports.

Another tool for nonprofits to strengthen their financial resolve is borrowing or obtaining a line of credit. Nonprofits are generally hesitant to discuss this option, as they naturally shy away from any kind of debt. However, it is important to adopt a business mindset when it comes to your organization's financial health; sometimes you need a line of credit to help with cash flow. If you have a federal or state-awarded grant, you must sometimes wait a long time for the reimbursement to arrive. A line of credit can help to smooth out those cash flow challenges and fluctuations.

Tool 5: Monitor budget performance and mission metrics

A critical piece of the budgeting equation is ensuring that you have good visibility into how you are performing against budget. As we have seen (and will discuss in greater detail in the next chapter), the need for accurate and timely reporting against your budget is paramount so that you and your team can make decisions when adjustments are necessary.

Depending on the complexity of the organization, various stakeholders, such as managers or department heads, will want to understand how their department is performing relative to their specific budget, while the leadership team will be more interested in the holistic view: "We might have variances and be slightly over here and slightly under there, but how are we doing from a big picture perspective? Are we over budget? If so, why?" Timely reporting will increase fiscal efficiency by helping you understand the "why" behind the figures.

The board will also want to ensure that the management team's operations are in line with what the board has approved. Finally, your funders will want to see how their dollars are being spent and that the organization is allocating those funds in accordance with the representations it made initially.

Monitoring your budget performance provides you with essential checks and balances. A second set of eyes can make sure any discrepancies are investigated and understood. But how often should this analysis be done – monthly, quarterly, or annually?

Each organization should set policies around how frequently different types of information are issued to various stakeholders. For example, how frequently do department managers receive budget-to-actuals for their department? How often does the senior leadership team and board receive budget-to-actuals for the overall organization? Ultimately, these decisions and the various reporting cadences come down to a balance between the resources an organization has available to perform the work and the frequency with which the various reports are desired.

In addition to monitoring the budget from a purely financial point of view, it is important to check income and expenses against the organization's key performance indicators (KPIs). You want to stay as closely aligned with your mission as possible, but how are you measuring that alignment, and how are you presenting the organization's progress to outside prospects, outside funders, and the board? Your KPIs should be a clear indicator of how the organization is investing its resources.

If you are measuring the number of lunches or after-school snacks you serve, for example, that should be a key focus of your monitoring program. If your funders are measuring your success on student growth or repeat youth engagement in a program, or the number of people you are getting to register to vote, those metrics should drive your reporting.

Tool 6: Mitigate risks with conservative budgeting

Nonprofits commonly encounter several challenges when planning and budgeting. One is caused by not budgeting early enough or looking far enough into the future. Another results from assuming a certain revenue level that doesn't ultimately materialize and having to make last-minute strategic decisions about what to eliminate or where to cut back.

Flexibility, on the other hand, is important for nonprofit organizations. We have discussed the importance of the reserve fund and line of credit concepts in preserving optionality, so the organization can respond to unexpected events and retain the ability to adjust its programs and spending while continuing to implement its mission. This is particularly the case when most of your revenue comes in the form of restricted or conditional grants, which can tie your hands and pose considerable challenges in this respect.

Another way to mitigate risks is to be fiscally conservative during the budgeting process and monitor how closely you stick to that budget throughout the year. Drafting a tight budget is one thing; adhering to it in practice is quite another. The most common way organizations get into trouble is when funding that was anticipated ("as good as in the bank") suddenly disappears. In other words, verbal pledges, expressions of interest, or draft proposals should not be budgeted as guaranteed revenue. This situation could arise if a funder changes priorities, the donor's circumstances shift, a matching grant is not met, or even due to an internal miscommunication between development and finance about the status of a pledge.

Not only should you be conservative, but you should own being conservative. Document your "conservative assumptions" page in the budget deck so stakeholders understand what's purposely not counted. In other words, embrace and communicate your cautious budgeting position. It means intentionally underestimating revenue, not counting on certain gifts until they are fully secured, and building your budget around what is confirmed, not just hoped for. You will sleep better at night without the emotional ups and downs of worrying whether you will be able to make payroll next month if a major funder does not come through.

Making planning and budgeting a collaborative process is also a key risk mitigation strategy. When senior leaders actively participate in setting their budgets, they are far more likely to take ownership and remain accountable. The more ownership leaders have, the less likely the organization is to drift off track financially.

Personnel is typically the largest expense for most organizations. That makes it especially important to avoid over-hiring, giving raises or bonuses outside of the approved budget, or expanding a team prematurely. Any of these actions can cause cascading issues for your organization in the future.

Another useful budgeting tool is using predefined triggers to guide your hiring or programmatic expansion. For example, if your student enrollment exceeds a certain threshold, such as 125 students per grade, you might need to add another section of sixth grade to maintain your student–teacher ratio. Or, if your earned revenue team generates more than $250,000 in the first quarter, you may choose to add another earned revenue team member during the second quarter. When clearly defined and revisited regularly, triggers can act as helpful guardrails that support responsible, flexible budgeting. Triggers turn heated budget debates into pre-agreed rules.

Tool 7: Apply planning principles to private foundations

When it comes to planning and budgeting for private foundations, most of the same principles hold true as with traditional nonprofit organizations. Unlike more traditional nonprofits, private foundations largely generate their revenue from investment income and asset appreciation, which they use to fund operations and make grants. The same approach of starting the budgeting process earlier and being fiscally conservative applies to private foundations. Private foundations should also ensure that the expenditure they commit to (staff, operational costs, and grants) for a particular budget year is aligned with the foundation's overall mission and objectives.

Summary

- **Accurate planning and budgeting are essential:** They enable nonprofits to align resources with their mission through a forward-thinking approach and careful balancing of core activities with new initiatives.

- **Mission alignment is crucial:** It is essential to establish a North Star to guide decisions and ensure that funding aligns with the organization's mission without compromising its focus.

- **Collaboration is key:** The budgeting process should involve collaboration with key stakeholders, including senior managers and the board, to ensure buy-in and transparent decision-making. This helps avoid misunderstandings and ensures that resources are allocated to achieve long-term impact, while remaining flexible to changing circumstances.

- **A reserve fund is highly desirable:** Nonprofits should aim to set aside a rainy-day fund to provide a buffer against unexpected challenges and ensure financial sustainability.

- **Timely and transparent reporting is fundamental:** Monitoring budget performance requires timely reporting and transparency across departments, leadership, and funders, which enables informed decision-making and fiscal efficiency. Regular variance analysis and alignment with organizational KPIs help track progress and mitigate risks, such as unanticipated revenue shortfalls or excessive spending.

FIVE
Accounting And Reporting

S trong accounting and reporting practices are at the heart of your role as a fiduciary, whether you are an executive director, CEO, COO, or board member. Your responsibilities include overseeing, managing, and reporting on your organization's financial performance to its various internal and external stakeholders. External stakeholders may include foundations, high-net-worth individuals, and government entities, while internal stakeholders include your leadership team and budget owners. For philanthropists and foundation staff, understanding nonprofit financial reporting is equally essential to evaluating grantee performance and supporting responsible stewardship.

Accuracy and timeliness in accounting and reporting are fundamental to your organization and essential to instilling confidence in all stakeholders. Without them, you risk losing existing funders, failing to attract new funders, alienating auditors and external tax preparers, and, if the situation deteriorates significantly through repeated noncompliance or financial mismanagement, even jeopardizing your nonprofit status.

Accounting and reporting are, in a way, the culmination of everything we discussed in the previous chapters, including internal controls, grants management practices, planning and budgeting, and cash management (which we will cover in the next chapter). Those elements are interconnected, and having them all in place is necessary to ensure success in your accounting and reporting efforts.

Effective financial leadership requires clarity, discipline, and a commitment to treating the nonprofit as a business as much as a mission-driven organization. Nonprofits are stewards of donor resources. Transparency, accountability, and strong systems aren't optional; they are core to protecting mission and trust.

Tool 1: Know the rules (GAAP + fund accounting)

Like any business, nonprofits are bound by GAAP, as established by the Financial Accounting Standards Board (FASB). In addition, organizations may have to satisfy other reporting requirements, including those stipulated at the state level, based on their indus-try, or due to grant conditions imposed by a funder. Nonprofits in the education sector, for instance, are typically subject to the requirements of their state authorizer, which might specify the chart of accounts the organization must use, for example.

A major factor that differentiates nonprofit accounting from more traditional accounting processes is the way grants must be accounted for, as we saw in Chapter 3. It is important for nonprofit organizations to have access to grants management accounting expertise to accurately reflect in the organization's financials how it is performing. Incorporating fund accounting, whereby restricted revenues and expenses are tracked separately and matched appropriately, will allow your organization to maintain accurate and orderly finan-cial statements and easily prepare reports for funders on how their funds have been spent.

It is not generally necessary to maintain separate bank accounts for each restricted grant unless a funder or government agency explicitly requires it. Opening twenty bank accounts for twenty restricted grants isn't efficient and can create significant administrative challenges in tracking your funds. Instead, if your organization uses a general operating bank account that includes restricted funds, you should track and reconcile all fund accounting within your accounting software to maintain an accurate picture of your finan-cial position. An alternative is to maintain a dedicated restricted-funds bank account and only transfer funds to your general operating account once the conditions tied to a particular grant have been met.

Tool 2: Use the right financial statements

There are three principal types of financial statements: the statement of financial position, the statement of activities, and the statement of cash flows. The first two are the most frequently referenced.

The statement of financial position is the organization's balance sheet, while the statement of activities is your profit and loss or income statement. Together, these two financial statements provide insights into the organization's financial performance, each statement offering a different focus.

The statement of financial position presents the organization's financial position, including its assets and liabilities as of a certain date, often the end of a month, quarter, or year. In contrast, the statement of activities shows how the organization performs over time, typically measured monthly, quarterly, or annually.

The statement of cash flows provides other valuable insights into the health of the organization by showing how it is using and replenishing its cash over time. It shows historical cash inflows and outflows. Pair that history with projected cash-flow estimates to assess whether anticipated revenue and planned expenses support operations in the coming month, quarter, or year.

Cash and cash flow are the lifeblood of any organization, and carefully monitoring both is imperative to successfully running your organization. Overall, the statement of financial position, the statement of activities, and the statement of cash flows provide different insights into your organization, and it is important to evaluate them collectively rather than each in isolation.

Tool 3: Recognize revenue and expenses correctly

There are three primary buckets of revenue:

1. Gifts (such as donations and many grants, depending on donor intent).

2. Earned revenue, which is typically revenue generated by an organization for services that the organization performs.

3. Other income, which includes interest and dividend income, investment income, and donated services.

Each revenue type has its own unique characteristics.

As we discussed in Chapter 3, grants can be restricted or unrestricted (often referred to as general operating funds) and can be conditional or unconditional. Different types of restrictions and conditions can be applied to a grant: for example, a restriction can be limited to a particular program or objective, geography, type of expense, or timeframe, while a grant may be conditional on the organization meeting specific milestones or deliverables before funding is released or recognized. In contrast, unrestricted grants have no such performance requirements and are generally recognized when received.

All those examples ultimately determine how the revenue from a particular grant is recognized. Is the grant revenue recognized up front at the time of receipt? Is the grant revenue only recognized as qualifying expenses are incurred? In the case of a two-year grant, is half the revenue recognized this year and half next year? These are the types of questions your finance and accounting teams should ask (and this is far from an exhaustive list).

When it comes to earned revenue, there are again different ways in which it can be generated and, in turn, recognized. For example, if an organization provides services to a school over the course of a school year and receives a lump-sum payment at the beginning of the year, the revenue should be recognized over time as the services are delivered, rather than all at once upon receipt.

The revenue recognition approach would be quite different if the organization provided a service for a one-time event, then invoiced for that event, and finally received payment. In that case, the revenue would be recognized upon billing or completion of the service.

"As a nonprofit, you need to be mindful of generating earned revenue from activities that are unrelated to the exempt purpose of your organization, known as unrelated business income tax (UBIT), since the organization may need to pay taxes on those revenues."
Ana Morgado, Controller,
Civic News Company

For other income, there are various factors to consider. For donated services, as an example, has the organization collected an invoice or supporting documentation from the service provider, and can it substantiate the amount the service provider claims was donated to the organization? For investment gains or losses, when securities are donated to the organization, how does the organization book a gain or loss on the sale of those securities? For bonds in which the organization has invested and which pay interest at maturity, have the appropriate accruals been booked based on the terms of the bond during the life of the investment? These are just a few accounting challenges that can emerge with other income sources.

As for expenses, they need to be recorded when they are incurred. If, for example, your organization is paying now for an event that is not due to take place for six months, the payment should not be recognized as an expense until the expense is actually incurred.

In contrast, when an organization purchases an asset that provides value over multiple years, such as a vehicle, equipment, or building, the accounting treatment depends on the organization's capitalization policies and procedures. Assets exceeding the capitalization threshold outlined in your accounting policies must be capitalized and depreciated (or amortized) over their useful life in accordance with GAAP. Those falling below the threshold should be expensed in the period of purchase.

Tool 4: Tailor financial communication to your audience

Your finance team should focus on customer service and provide the appropriate information to your various stakeholders promptly so they can make informed decisions. Accuracy is paramount. The fastest way for a finance team to undermine its credibility and stakeholders' confidence is by making mistakes. One error will raise the question, "Where else has the finance team made mistakes?"

Your finance team's communications approach is also critical. Often, finance teams think, "We know finance. We know accounting. It's our responsibility to prepare the financial statements and release them. Then our job is done." That assumption overlooks the fact that not everyone else understands finance and accounting in the same way. What is as clear as day to the finance team is often the complete opposite to the recipients of their materials.

The finance team must tailor its message to its audience, whether that is the organization's executive leadership team, the CEO, the executive director, or the board, and distill the critical pieces of information into easily digestible bites. The board will typically consist of individuals from various backgrounds, including members of the community with little to no finance experience. If those board members cannot interpret or use the financial information to make informed decisions, the finance team hasn't done its job.

One effective approach is to pair the financials with clear notes explaining major variances from the budget or the year prior. For example, "We spent four times more on consultants this year because we were unable to hire full-time staff to fill our open positions," or whatever the reason. The same applies to balance sheet items. Any financial numbers that stand out should be explained. If your finance team is presenting financial results, they should be prepared to walk the audience through key line items and any material variances from the budget. Financials should not be a mystery; everyone should understand what is going on.

You must also report in a timely manner and standardized format to your budget owners. You might believe that your organization is not large enough to need anything other than a consolidated reporting package and that producing separate reports for each department or division is an unnecessary complication, but the reason for issuing more granular reports to your departments or divisions is to help the budget owners manage their budgets and also ensure more eyes review the financials to catch anything that might require further investigation.

The more transparency you can provide, the better. This is a critical piece of the puzzle that is often overlooked or ignored.

Tool 5: Pair financial reporting with program impact

Reporting on your organization's programmatic impact is critical not only for holding yourself and your organization accountable but also for providing confirmation to your community, funders, board, and others that what you are doing is working. What was the status of the constituents your organization is serving before your involvement? What was your approach or the process you implemented to address the issues you are trying to improve or solve, and how much improvement did your constituents experience because of your involvement? These are the questions you should look to answer as you formulate your plan for conveying the impact your organization is having on its constituent population.

You will also want to measure how efficiently your organization is serving its constituents. If, for example, your organization serves 100,000 individuals and has an annual budget of $3 million, its estimated "cost to serve" is $30 per individual. (Cost to serve can be a simple metric to help assess scale and efficiency.) If, five years later, your organization is serving a million individuals and the budget is $5 million, the cost to serve has decreased to $5 per individual, which shows that the organization has become far more efficient at serving its constituents.

It cannot be emphasized enough how important it is for you to be able to clearly quantify and report to your stakeholders the impact your organization has on the community it serves. Ultimately, foundations and funders want results. They want to know the effectiveness of the programs they are funding and that your organization is doing its utmost to make those programs successful, achieve its goals, and realize its mission.

Tool 6: Report strategically to your board

As you are aware, all nonprofits have a board of directors (the exception being a charitable project or program housed within a fiscal sponsor). It is essential that you establish a good working relationship with your board, as they are, in effect, your boss. At the same time, it is helpful to keep in mind that board members are typically volunteers, giving their time and expertise without compensation. Showing appreciation for their service will help you develop a positive working relationship with them.

How you report your financials to your board depends on the structure of the board. For boards with established finance and/or audit committees, most of the finance team's interactions will be with members of those two committees, which will then report the appropriate financial information to the board. For boards that do not have a committee structure, the finance team will report directly to the board or its treasurer.

In either case, the board must ensure that the organization is appropriately safeguarding its assets, managing its budget, and monitoring its cash flow and cash reserves. The board will use the approved budget as a key reference point, often through budget-to-actual variance analysis, to measure the organization's progress over the year.

The finance committee and/or treasurer should act as an additional set of eyes and ears to protect the organization's financial viability. They should, for example, ensure that the organization requires expenditures over a certain threshold to have treasurer approval and that the board treasurer approves the CEO's expenses. Since the CEO reports to the board, it would be inappropriate for somebody on the management team to approve the CEO's expenses.

Boards play a critical role beyond governance formalities. They must ask questions, support leadership, uphold fiduciary standards, and ensure the organization remains operationally strong without overstepping into daily management.

As for the frequency of reporting to the board, meetings should generally be at least quarterly (or as specified by your bylaws or the requirements of those entities governing your organization). At times, meeting more frequently may be beneficial to you and your board. If so, you should ensure that your board members understand why you recommend holding additional meetings and what the intended outcome of those is. Whatever cadence is chosen, plan meetings well in advance and keep the schedule consistent so that your board knows what to expect and can prioritize their attendance.

Tool 7: Maintain a consistent reporting calendar

Consistency also applies to other financial tasks, such as reconciliations, which need to be done monthly. Depending on the strength of your organization's balance sheet and days' cash on hand, your organization may need to reconcile more frequently to ensure that the most important expenses (including payroll) are prioritized, given your current cash balances or funds coming into the organization. Maintaining trackers and calendars helps to keep everybody focused on the required deliverables. It is also important to ensure continuity by cross-training staff, so that if somebody is on vacation, off sick, or suddenly leaves the organization, the whole finance and accounting ecosystem does not grind to a halt.

Of course, adhering to a reporting calendar can be difficult when board members, the development team, or funders request ad hoc analyses from the finance team (and every such analysis is deemed "urgent"). Often, day-to-day financial and accounting work is deprioritized in favor of these ad hoc requests. If this is the case, the leader of the finance and accounting team must determine how time-sensitive and critical the asks are and push back (gently) on the less urgent and important requests. Perhaps information that the finance team has already generated can satisfy the request, or there is a simpler way of producing the requested information that checks the box. It can be beneficial to have all such requests funneled through one person, who serves as a gatekeeper and protects the rest of the finance team. Time is your scarcest resource. Protect it.

After accuracy, timeliness is the second most critical requirement in reporting. If the person responsible for processing accounts payable fails to do their job for two months, it will have serious cascading implications. Not only might your vendors stop working with you because they haven't been paid, but your financials will not accurately represent reality because there are invoices that haven't been entered into the accounting system.

Conversely, if the person responsible for accounts receivable isn't issuing invoices for work that has been done, the organization might be losing a critical revenue stream that is desperately needed to keep the organization's operations afloat.

Tool 8: Upgrade systems as you scale

Solutions like Excel, Google Sheets, and QuickBooks continue to work well for most smaller organizations, but as your organization grows and its level of complexity increases, more sophisticated accounting software may be needed, which can also facilitate reporting and strengthen internal controls.

Subscription costs for accounting platforms can vary significantly. A solid, entry-level accounting package like QuickBooks typically starts around $1,200 per year, depending on the features and number of users. More advanced systems like Sage Intacct can exceed $20,000 annually, and that figure often excludes any additional customization required to meet the organization's specific needs.

Summary

- **Strong accounting and reporting are essential:** To fulfill your fiduciary duty, instill trust among stakeholders, and ensure continued funding and nonprofit status, accurate and timely financial reporting is a *sine qua non* and reflects sound internal controls and overall organizational health.

- **Nonprofit accounting must align with GAAP:** This includes fund accounting, which tracks revenue and expenses by restriction or purpose (e.g., restricted versus unrestricted funds), and compliance with grant-specific requirements, such as ensuring funds are used only for approved programs and recognizing revenue based on conditions or restrictions.

- **Financial statements should be reviewed together:** Each different financial statement tells only part of the financial story; together, these statements support decision-making and help assess financial health. They must be supplemented by clear, tailored communication.

- **Good communication is paramount:** Finance teams must communicate clearly and proactively with stakeholders, especially non-finance audiences like board members and program staff. Breaking down complex data, explaining variances, and offering timely, relevant insights builds confidence and fosters informed decision-making.

- **It is important to use the right tools:** Maintaining a reporting calendar and ensuring cross-functional training protects accuracy and timeliness while managing ad hoc demands. As an organization grows, adopting more advanced accounting software can streamline operations and improve reporting efficiency.

SIX

Cash Management

C ash is often described as "king." For most organizations, the single largest use of cash is payroll. Ensuring there is sufficient cash to make payroll is the number-one priority in managing cash flow.

In connection with this chapter, I spoke with Robert Price, Chief Financial Officer at Ascend Schools, who has spent most of his career as a corporate controller, VP of finance, or CFO, and came to the nonprofit space as a CFO in 2015. He immediately emphasized the priority of making payroll.

"Whether you're a nonprofit or for-profit,
you must be able to make payroll. This is a lesson
I learned when working with venture

*capital-funded start-ups, where getting caught
without enough money to make payroll between
fundings was a constant fear."*
Robert Price, Chief Financial Officer,
Ascend Schools

Beyond that, having a strong cash management plan can make life much easier for the organization. Constantly worrying about making payroll, paying bills, and not having sufficient leeway to think strategically about realizing the organization's mission or the projects it is meant to undertake is highly stressful and distracting. "Are we going to run out of money midstream on this project?" is a question you don't want to be asking yourself.

Good cash management gives you reassuring visibility and predictability around how the organization will fund its expenses during a particular period, so that leadership can focus on the bigger picture and mission-critical priorities.

---

*"Effective cash management allows management
to focus on the mission of the organization,
knowing that projects won't be interrupted
because of a lack of funding."*
Robert Price

Part and parcel of a strong cash management strategy is having a Plan B, and ideally a Plan C and a Plan D, in case circumstances change unexpectedly. We discussed the importance of such an emergency plan in Chapter 4, as well as the value of having a rainy-day or reserve fund, which is also a cornerstone of any cash management plan. The goal for any organization is to build a reserve fund and never have to use it. However, if an organization does need to use its reserve fund, it knows it has that option and that it will live to fight another day.

Tool 1: Build a rolling cash flow forecast

One key element of effective cash management is projecting cash flow over time. While some organizations forecast for the full fiscal year and update projections monthly, others rely on shorter rolling forecasts (e.g., thirteen-week models) to maintain near-term visibility and responsiveness. Either way, the goal is to track monthly inflows and outflows. Outflows are typically easier to project – you likely know your payroll obligations, rent, and recurring expenses such as travel and supplies. These known costs make it easier to estimate your future spending with reasonable accuracy.

On the other side of the equation, you (hopefully) have a combination of cash on hand and anticipated cash receipts, whether from gifts or any earned revenue associated with the organization's work. These two elements should serve as a roadmap showing where your organization is headed from month to month and will either project confidence in your numbers and your organization's financial position or, conversely, allow you to anticipate where you will run into problems in the future. In such a case, you can either recalibrate your expenses or ensure that there is more revenue coming in the door at that time.

"You can often adjust your expenses when cash gets tight, but your cash inflows are harder to control. That's why it's critical to understand and closely monitor your cash receipts."
Robert Price

If the organization has a large accounts payable balance, it will also need to be factored into the cash management equation. Calculating run rates and steady-state expense levels is all very well, but if the organization has a significant backlog of unpaid bills, they must be included in any cash flow analysis.

For example, to create a cash flow forecast for a nonprofit with an operating budget of $5–10 million, Robert Price recommends reviewing the following data as a starting point:

1. Number of days' operating expenses covered by unrestricted cash on hand.

2. Average payroll, including employer taxes, and when this is paid (e.g., the fifteenth and last day of the month; bi-weekly).

3. Average employee benefits cost (e.g., medical, life, disability, retirement plan).

4. "First of the month" payments (e.g., rent, utilities, telephone and internet, debt or loan payments).

5. Any seasonal payments coming due (e.g., annual insurance renewals that aren't financed, annual software subscriptions).

6. Current balance and aging of outstanding accounts payable.

7. Seasonality of contributions, if any, and a review of the weighted pipeline for expected gift revenue.

8. Any expected earned revenue and/or other income.

9. Amount and aging of any receivables.

10. Status of line of credit (i.e., what is the unused portion?).

Once you have this data, you should prepare a six-month cash forecast, ideally by week for the first twelve weeks and then by month for the following three months.

You should also consider implementing the following points as you manage your cash flow:

- When cash flow permits and funder restrictions allow, pay vendors slightly ahead of terms to build goodwill for future situations when you may need to delay payment.

- Evaluate whether spreading your insurance premiums over monthly or quarterly installments could help preserve cash, even if it results in a small financing fee.

- Buy used office furniture: it is often a quarter of the cost, but most of it is only a year old. No one cares how fancy your desk is.

- Go light on leasehold improvements; make it nice, but it doesn't need to be the Ritz-Carlton. Spend that money on your employees.

- Evaluate leasing tech equipment, particularly equipment you replace every three or four years.

- Look out for the nickels and dimes.

"A large nursing home operator with 100,000 beds nationwide served three meals per day. They worked out that if they could save two cents per meal per day, that would translate into more than $2 million in savings!"
Robert Price

As your organization grows, it can harness economies of scale.

Tool 2: Balance liquidity and growth

General best practice recommends maintaining at least ninety days of cash on hand, though the appropriate reserve level depends on your organization's funding volatility and program commitments. The more cash on hand your organization has, the more flexibility it has with its financial resources. For instance, if you calculate that your organization has only three or four months of operating cash, maintaining liquidity will be essential. But if you have six to nine months of reserves, you may be able to strategically redeploy excess funds into higher-yielding investments subject to board oversight.

For example, organizations with stable revenue streams, such as charter schools and certain health-care providers, should aim to maintain at least ninety days of operating expenses, plus projected annual capital expenditures, in cash on hand. In contrast, organizations that rely heavily on philanthropy and lack a sizable endowment should target at least 180 days of cash reserves.

"Regardless of the type of organization you are running, try to have at least thirty days' operating expenses available on an unused line of credit."
Robert Price

As we have discussed, reserve funds are primarily funds that you have set aside for a rainy day, but those funds also provide additional optionality for the organization and could, for example, be invested longer term in the hope of picking up some additional yield. If an organization is striving for a six-month reserve, for example, and also has good visibility into its twelve-month budget in the current fiscal year, then those six months of reserves can be invested in short-term, low-risk vehicles consistent with your organization's policy.

Conversely, the picture is different if an organization has only a two-month reserve fund and ninety days' cash on hand, because there is a high probability that the organization will need to tap into its reserve fund at some point during its current budget year, perhaps within the next three to four months, in which case those reserve funds should remain highly liquid, limiting the organization's options for growth.

The opportunity cost of not having a well-thought-out cash management strategy is significantly higher today than it was in the past. When US interest rates hovered near zero, the potential gains from strategic investing were negligible. Simply sitting on idle cash can be highly detrimental to your organization. For example, if you have $1 million earning 4% in a money market account, that is an additional $40,000 in annual income without asking anyone for a donation. But if that $1 million is sitting in a non-interest-bearing bank account, you are effectively forgoing $40,000 in revenue.

I have seen organizations with several million dollars of cash sitting in a bank account, earning two basis points (0.02%). For a $3-million cash balance, the organization was earning approximately $50 a month in interest. Switching those funds to a money market account, which yielded approximately 4% at the time, meant that the $3 million generated approximately $10,000 in interest a month (rates will vary based on market conditions). One simple change resulted in close to $120,000 in additional annual income for the organization. (Note that money-market funds are not FDIC-insured; money-market deposit accounts at banks may be, subject to limits.)

While large nonprofits and foundations often have a formal Investment Policy Statement (IPS), many early-stage and midsized nonprofits instead address investment and cash handling practices in their financial policies manual or treasury procedures. Wherever these policies live, the board is responsible under UPMIFA (the Uniform Prudent Management of Institutional Funds Act) for ensuring the organization invests prudently, preserves liquidity, and maintains appropriate controls. As organizations grow and reserves increase, formalizing a standalone IPS becomes best practice.

Tool 3: Manage risk with conservative investing

As we have seen, having emergency plans in place and setting aside a reserve fund are the two principal elements of any risk management strategy. Cash management is also about thinking through and detailing your anticipated expenses and revenues to protect the organization as much as possible from cash shortfalls.

"Expenses shouldn't be unexpected; neither should revenue shortfalls. ABF: always be forecasting!"
Robert Price

It is also about being cautious in your investment strategy, which should always err on the side of conservatism rather than aggression. The more safety nets your organization establishes, the more fiscally secure it will ultimately be.

Before embarking on a strategy that involves locking up funds for a particular period, you should ensure that your investment approach mirrors the realities of the organization. For example, if your organization has visibility on sixty days' cash on hand in its current operating budget and a reserve of two months, it would be foolish to buy a six-month Treasury bill or CD – the organization would effectively restrict access to those funds for a period of six months, when in reality you may need them in three or four months.

"Nonprofits that are dependent on philanthropy should invest as conservatively as possible. The investment policy should stress protection of

*principal, which means that investments should
be safe (e.g., in Treasury bills) and short-term
(i.e., 30–90-day maturities). Long-term investments
(>180 days) should be made only with funds not
required for at least one year."*
Robert Price

Even if you do have "excess" funds to invest, caution is the watchword. Nonprofits are generally not set up to speculate or otherwise expose themselves to market risk; the goal is to preserve and protect the funds that have been given or granted to the organization. The same applies when an individual or foundation donates shares of stock or any other asset. Typically, those assets should be liquidated immediately.

One relatively safe investment option, however, is a CD ladder. This takes advantage of the FDIC insurance limit, which protects up to $250,000 per depositor, per insured bank, per ownership category. Let's say that your organization has $1 million that it can invest for up to twelve months. Instead of tying up the whole amount for twelve months, however, and leaving $750,000 uninsured if the bank failed before maturity, you could divide it into four tranches of $250,000 and buy CDs at four different banks. That way, $1 million is completely FDIC-insured, and you have eliminated the risk of any one bank getting into trouble and being unable to pay off your CD when it matures.

In addition, you might buy three-, six-, nine-, and twelve-month CDs at each of the four banks to ensure that the organization has continuous liquidity after the initial three-month period. Thus, in three months, you would have $250,000 to spend, and after six months, a further $250,000, and so on. As each tranche matures, you will be able to make a new decision as to what to do with those funds; continue the ladder and buy another CD or, if things have changed at the organization because, for example, you didn't get one of the grants you had anticipated, you can keep those funds in cash until you have better long-term visibility on your cash situation.

Another tool we discussed earlier is to open a line of credit, which can help organizations manage the ebbs and flows of their operating business and, therefore, their capital requirements and cash needs, assuming the economics are appropriate and the fees are not excessive. Here, again, a conservative approach is the order of the day.

"Have a sub-limit feature under your line of credit for the issuance of letters of credit (LOC). This allows the line to serve as the collateral, as opposed to having to make a dollar-for-dollar deposit to back up the LOC."
Robert Price

Tool 4: Ground projections in reality

People often enter the nonprofit world because they have bold ambitions and idealistic goals. While that passion is essential, it can unintentionally create challenges when it comes to financial discipline. CEOs and executive directors may presume that generous grants will arrive or push for ambitious new programs based on enthusiasm rather than confirmed funding. One of the finance team's key responsibilities is to gently challenge those assumptions, ground decisions in reality, and ensure that financial stewardship aligns with, but is not overrun by, the organization's mission.

Development teams, too, tend to operate with optimistic projections about future donations and grants. That optimism can be a tremendous asset, but finance's job is to introduce a degree of caution and structure, ensuring that projections are achievable and aligned with current operational realities.

Timing, in particular, is an area where misalignment often occurs. Development may say, "If a major donation comes in July rather than March, it's no big deal, is it? We still get the donation." But for finance, timing is everything. That delay could mean the organization doesn't make payroll in May. The stakes for the finance team are much higher – while others can afford to be off by a few months, finance must ensure the organization has sufficient cash on hand when it is needed.

This ultimately comes back to careful budgeting, of course, but the most critical aspect is managing cash and cash flow. Finance must go beyond static budget numbers to understand and forecast when cash will actually arrive and when it needs to go out. A well-balanced budget will not prevent a crisis if the organization runs out of money mid-year because funds arrived later than expected. That is why cash flow modeling and projecting inflows and outflows month by month are among the most essential tools in nonprofit financial management.

"One of the major traps nonprofits fall into is not investing in the right finance management staff. You need someone with experience and the ability to navigate challenging conversations to push back on pie-in-the-sky philanthropy projections, over-hiring, and spending in front of revenue."
Robert Price

As discussed in earlier chapters, organizations need to be particularly mindful of how restricted funds are managed. They require a different approach from unrestricted funds because they must not be released until they meet the funder's criteria. Organizations cannot spend restricted funds earmarked for a specific initiative on anything that hasn't been designated by the donor. They need an organized system to document and manage those restricted funds to stay compliant with their grant agreements and the requirements of an audit.

Finally, you must ensure that your organization always maintains appropriate levels of liquidity. It can be cash-flush, with two or three years of cash on hand, which other organizations might only dream of having, but if you haven't thought through the liquidity needs of that cash and have locked it up so that it is inaccessible when the organization needs it, you might as well not have it.

Tool 5: Use simple tools and strong processes

Depending on your organization's complexity and level of sophistication, various software and accounting packages can assist with your cash management, although simple technologies such as Excel and Google Sheets have stood the test of time and are still a generally reliable solution for most organizations.

"If you are a very large institution, such as a college or university with a billion-dollar-plus endowment, there are certainly advanced technologies that could prove helpful. However, for most nonprofits, a simple Excel spreadsheet or Google Sheet is typically sufficient."
Robert Price

No technology will help, however, if the organization is in disarray or experiences such rapid staff turnover that no one is consistently overseeing financial operations. More important than any software solution for the challenges we have discussed is having continuity and policies and procedures in place to ensure that the organization actually does whatever it is committed to doing. Indeed, the best "technology" is simply being methodical and committed to staying organized.

Tool 6: Apply cash principles to private foundations

Unlike traditional nonprofit organizations that typically prioritize short- to medium-term liquidity to support ongoing programs and operations and often invest more conservatively (e.g., in CDs, bonds, and treasuries), private foundations focus largely on long-term capital preservation and growth objectives to sustain giving over many decades. Many private foundations allocate assets to alternative investments (e.g., private equity and hedge funds) due to fewer liquidity constraints. Private foundations must still manage the liquidity of their asset base to ensure that appropriate cash levels are maintained to fund operations and grant commitments.

Summary

- **Cash flow management is critical:** Ensuring sufficient cash to meet payroll should always be a top priority.

- **Effective cash management reduces stress:** It allows organizations to focus on their mission and strategic projects without constantly worrying about funding gaps.

- **Detailed forecasting is a must:** A strong cash management strategy includes creating rolling cash flow forecasts, factoring in regular expenses and payables, and maintaining a reserve fund for unexpected shortfalls.

- **Build and protect a reserve fund:** Organizations should aim to maintain at least ninety days of cash on hand for operations (and 180 days for those reliant largely on philanthropy), with liquidity being key to flexibility.

- **Conservatism is the order of the day:** Cash management involves being conservative in investments, using safe options like CDs, and having emergency plans to manage risks and ensure financial stability.

SEVEN

Tax Returns And Audits

When it comes to taxation, nonprofits receive several important benefits, the most important being an exemption from corporate tax and the ability for donors to make tax-deductible contributions. In exchange for those benefits, the organization is required by the IRS and state agencies to file an annual tax return, typically Form 990, which is more detailed than a standard individual or corporate return. It includes financial statements, governance disclosures, compensation information, and details about programmatic activities. The goal is not only to verify compliance, but also to demonstrate transparency and accountability to the public.

In this tax filing, the organization must provide insights not only into its financials, but also into its mission and programs, its governance and lobbying activities, its funding and spending, and any compensation paid to board members and others. You should be aware that 501(c)(3)s cannot engage in partisan political activity and may only conduct limited lobbying.

These returns are also made public (on the IRS website and other websites) so that anyone, including potential donors, can understand how the organization operates and assess its stewardship. In this way, the IRS can enforce compliance, and the public can exercise oversight.

Nonprofits must therefore ensure that their tax filings are complete and accurate and that their financials are in order. The longer a nonprofit exists, the more opportunities the IRS has to examine its filings, especially if red flags appear. If that happens, the organization must have all supporting documentation readily available. If you cannot provide it, the IRS may assess fines and penalties and, in extreme cases, revoke tax-exempt status. Separately, if a Form 990 return is not filed for three consecutive years, the IRS will automatically revoke tax-exempt status, which can be costly and time-consuming to restore.

In this chapter, we cover key federal and state filing requirements and the importance of annual audits, drawing on insights from Aaron Fox, CPA, National Not-For-Profit Tax Leader at CBIZ, and Gus Saliba, Partner at PKF O'Connor Davies.

"The nonprofit sector is one of the most scrutinized and transparent of all sectors."
Aaron Fox, National Not-For-Profit
Tax Leader, CBIZ

Understand your tax filing obligations

In addition to Form 990, the federal tax filing, your organization might have to file Form 990-T (Exempt Organization Business Income Tax Return) if gross unrelated business income is $1,000 or more in a tax year, state charitable registration filings (if it is a 501(c)(3) organization and is registered to solicit contributions), state incorporation renewal filings (to keep its incorporation status current), and local tax filings (for property, sales, and use tax responsibilities). Depending on the organization's mission and the initiatives in which it is involved, other tax filings may also be required.

Here we are principally concerned with the (federal) Form 990 filing.

Use Form 990 as a strategic document

Since this book is aimed at nonprofits with average receipts of at least $200,000 and assets of more than $500,000, we are concerned with tax return Form 990 (rather than Forms 990-N or 990-EZ, which are for smaller organizations), though we will also discuss briefly the tax requirements for private foundations, which must file a Form 990-PF. Most exempt organizations are required to e-file their Form 990 return.

As mentioned earlier, a nonprofit's 990 tax filing involves much more than declaring its profit and loss. It requires a wide range of other information, including answers to a whole battery of questions, such as: Who are the organization's officers? What was their compensation? Who is on the board? Were any of the board members compensated? Who are the major donors of the organization? How much did they give? Does the organization have in place various policies, including whistleblowing, conflict of interest, and data retention?

"The 990 is less a tax return and more an informational filing about the effectiveness of the nonprofit. It often requires programmatic, legal, board, and CFO input to complete."
Aaron Fox

In other words, completing a 990 is a cross-functional effort, not just a finance exercise. Form 990 includes Schedule A, which tests whether you continue to qualify as a public charity (versus becoming a private foundation). Management should brief the board on this test annually, so the board understands trends and any risks. If public-support percentages trend down, the board should discuss contingency plans (e.g., advance planning to avoid private-foundation reclassification).

Completing a 990 filing (and any other required tax filings) is not a simple undertaking. Your CFO and controller (or their equivalents) should work closely with a qualified nonprofit tax preparer to ensure full compliance. Often, this tax preparer will be from the same firm that handles your audit, which has the advantage of providing continuity and access to existing organizational information.

Start Form 990 preparation early

Preparing a full Form 990 takes time. Your team must compile data, your tax preparer must analyze it, and leadership and the board must review the return before filing. You will also want to ensure that management beyond the finance team and your board have an opportunity to review it. Form 990 is due by the 15th day of the 5th month after the fiscal year-end (e.g., May 15 for a December 31 year-end). You can request an automatic 6-month extension via Form 8868, but not for state filings unless separately permitted. An extension can be helpful, but it should not replace year-round preparation. The IRS can assess monetary penalties for late 990s even when no tax is due.

How far in advance you should start preparing your information before the 990 filing deadline depends on several factors, not the least of which is whether this will be the first or fifteenth 990 the organization has filed. If it is your first year of operations, it is wise to start well before your fiscal year ends because a lot of information that has nothing to do with the organization's financials is required, and the sooner you get started on that, the better. You will then have less work to do at the last minute when you are scrambling to put together your financials.

Once you have gone through the process of answering the litany of questions on the 990 for the first time, you will probably find that your responses will not change meaningfully from year to year, though there will certainly be sections that need to be updated as your business evolves. Your donor base may not be the same each year, for example, and your compensation will change, as will your agreements with independent contractors.

In any case, you should not wait until the year-end to think about the tax information needed for the form. Rather, have a process during the year to code accounts and pull aside the data that will be used for the 990. It becomes much less of a chore if it's prepared that way.

If your organization is performing a financial audit for the year, you might be tempted to wait until the audit is finished before starting the Form 990 process. That is one of the biggest mistakes nonprofits make.

"So much of the information disclosed in Form 990 is not dependent on the financial audit outcome,

and by waiting until the audit is closed to begin
work, you are putting yourself behind the eight
ball and making the tax preparation process
more frantic than it needs to be."
Aaron Fox

Many leading nonprofits have a dedicated person assigned to compliance needs, and that person works on this data year-round. Even if you don't have that kind of resource, you should emulate this process to the best of your ability by maintaining adequate documentation and records, as well as having a compliance calendar to track all your obligations.

Review Form 990 thoughtfully before approval

Once your tax preparer has completed the 990, it needs to be reviewed and approved before submission. The review process for established nonprofits should start with management, then your legal department, then your audit or finance committee, and finally the board. For newer or smaller nonprofits, the review process could be as simple as having the organization's tax preparer walk you through the filing before sending it to the board for their review.

Typically, within several months of filing your organization's 990 with the IRS, a version of it will appear online for public review. (For most 501(c)(3) public charities, donor names on Schedule B are redacted in the public-disclosure copy. Private foundations' Schedule B is public, and some states have their own disclosure rules.) This public disclosure can sometimes trigger unwanted responses, including articles based on the reported information. The 990 includes details such as business relationships and their associated costs, as well as executive compensation. Public access to this level of detail is simply a fact of life for nonprofit organizations.

You can also expect questions from bankers, donors, and other interested parties, so it is a good idea to be ready to respond intelligently to such requests.

As an ongoing organization, you will be subject to random examinations by the IRS and, sooner or later, an audit. If your financials are in order, this should be no cause for concern, though it is important to understand what they are looking for in an audit.

"With IRS examinations, it's important to establish a cooperative and friendly tone from the onset and to provide timely responses to their questions."
Aaron Fox

First and foremost, the IRS requires an organization to keep adequate documentation to support the 990 reporting, without which the IRS may rule that the organization no longer deserves exempt status.

Beyond that, the IRS will be looking for evidence of the misallocation of funds, whether because of intentional deception or simply poor governance. For example, if an organization has a million-dollar annual budget and spends $600,000 on fundraising and only $200,000 on programmatic initiatives, the IRS will see this as an anomaly and instigate an investigation. After all, the goal of any nonprofit is to have as many dollars as possible flow into its mission and programs, which is what its donors are looking to see.

On the other hand, reporting little or no fundraising expenses, especially if your organization shows high fundraising revenue, can raise red flags with the IRS, watchdog organizations, or the public. All nonprofits must invest in fundraising, and those costs should be appropriately reflected on the 990 to ensure transparency, avoid misinterpretation, and present a realistic picture of operations. None of these items automatically mean misconduct, but they increase the likelihood of IRS scrutiny, which is why consistent documentation and clear policies matter.

Other "red flags" the IRS is on the lookout for include:

1. Reporting salaries and wages for employees on the 990 but not filing corresponding IRS Form W-2s (wage and tax statements) and vice versa

2. Excessive compensation to staff and compensation to board members

3. Excessive unrelated business income (UBI)

4. Excessive lobbying activities

5. Large, unexplained negative balances or swings in revenue, expenses, or net assets

6. Unusual bonus arrangements

7. Large prior period adjustments

8. Amended filings

9. Late filings

10. Missed filings

"The IRS has its systems tuned to irregularities on Form 990 submissions and uses algorithms to select nonprofits for examination."
Aaron Fox

Because nonprofits are generally exempt from tax on mission-related income, they must be careful about activities that generate UBI, which is taxed at corporate rates. Excessive amounts of UBI can also jeopardize a nonprofit's exempt status.

Typical UBI activities may include advertising (not acknowledgments), debt-financed income, rental income when services are provided or from personal property, certain gaming, and sales of merchandise unrelated to mission. Passive rent from real property without services generally is not UBI unless debt-financed.

Navigate private foundation filing rules

Because they rely on an endowment to fuel their gifts and pay operating expenses, private foundations typically have complicated investment strategies, and even stricter rules apply to their tax filings. Various math tests are applied to Form 990-PF to make sure private foundations are distributing approximately 5% annually, complying with the jeopardizing-investments and self-dealing rules, and meeting excise-tax obligations on investment income. Even for seasoned tax preparers, 990-PFs are difficult to complete without substantial experience with private foundations and the relevant tax filing requirements. For that reason, most private foundations work with tax preparers who specialize in Form 990-PF and related rules.

Use audits to strengthen your organization

In Chapter 1, we briefly reviewed the benefits to your organization of performing an annual audit, how to approach an audit to ensure a positive working relationship with your auditor, and what can go wrong if your organization is unprepared for your audit.

Depending on your organization's size, the number of annual financial transactions, and the overall complexity of its finances, the cost of engaging an audit firm can often start at around $10,000. In addition, the audit process demands significant time and effort, particularly from management and the finance team. If your organization operates with a lean finance team that is already stretched thinly, adding an audit to the mix can be overwhelming.

When an audit is mandatory:

- If your organization expends $750,000 or more in federal awards in a fiscal year, a Single Audit under Uniform Guidance is required, even if a standard financial statement audit wouldn't otherwise be.

- Several states mandate audits, reviews, or compilations once annual revenue or charitable contributions exceed statutory thresholds. Check your state charitable registration requirements.

Yet, there are several reasons to perform an audit, even when it is not legally required. Once your organization reaches a certain size, it may be beneficial to conduct an audit to convey to your constituents that you have a sound financial structure. The organization's board might equally drive such an imprimatur as confirmation that the financial picture presented by management is representative of the organization's actual financial situation.

> *"Even when not required by statute, boards*
> *often seek the assurance and credibility*
> *that an independent audit provides."*
> Gus Saliba, Partner, PKF O'Connor Davies

A potential funder might require an audit as a condition of investing in the organization or releasing future funds to ensure a similar level of accountability and transparency to their own. The potential funder wants to ensure that your internal controls are sufficient to safeguard the funds they are about to disburse, that your numbers are not materially misstated, and that the organization will responsibly deploy their investment or gift. Certainly, if you are looking to raise more money, the lack of an audit could be a major handicap.

Whatever the reasons behind it, auditing ultimately helps to elevate your organization's stature. You can send the audit to prospective funders, put it on your website, and present it to the relevant authorities. In other words, you can use it to your advantage rather than regarding it as an annoyance.

Beyond all of that, you will almost certainly find your auditor helpful. For example, grant agreements can be unclear, so it is valuable to be able to ask your auditor to review a particularly confusing grant agreement and clarify any ambiguities or potential conflicts. Indeed, you shouldn't hesitate to reach out to your auditor for such assistance.

For all these reasons, it is worth having your organization's finances audited annually. Even though an audit may appear to involve additional expense and work, in the long run it can save you both, provided you are properly prepared, understand the process, and respond effectively to the auditor's findings.

Get the timing right

If your finance team is performing its responsibilities at a high level month in and month out, conducting an audit shouldn't be overwhelming for them. In addition, an audit shouldn't conflict with your end-of-year tax filing, which is typically prepared once the audit has concluded.

Ideally, you should formally start your audit within three or four months of the end of your financial year. Thus, if your fiscal year ends December 31, you should be in discussions with your auditor in January or February to establish the timeline for when you and your team will be able to provide the auditor with the information they need and formally start the audit.

Remember that an auditor may have hundreds of other clients. Therefore, it is important to agree with your auditor on how your collaboration will work so they can allocate the necessary resources internally and ensure their availability when you need them. Approaching auditors at the last minute is typically not a recipe for success.

This means that, with the assistance of you and your management team, your board (technically, your board contracts with the auditor) will need to start the process of selecting an auditor by putting together a list of potential firms and arranging interviews three or four months before the end of your fiscal year. You should target selecting an auditor at least a month before you intend to start working with them. In the above example, your board would select the auditor by the end of December.

Choose the right auditor

Your board should be looking for a firm that has worked with many nonprofits and, ideally, with non-profits in your industry. Does the prospective auditor have two or three clients in your sector, or do they have fifty or a hundred? The firm you choose should have deep nonprofit and sector experience, not just general audit expertise.

Occasionally, the state in which your organization is incorporated will have a list of recommended auditors, but you should still do your due diligence. Review the senior management of the audit firm and, above all, the firm's most recent peer review. Every firm must go through a peer review evaluation, which will tell you how another independent audit firm perceives them. Lastly, ask for references and follow up on those references.

Establishing a strong working relationship with your auditor is essential. Questions will undoubtedly arise during the year, and you want to be able to reach out to them with a question or to review your thought process around a particular issue. Are the firms your board has shortlisted likely to engage with you in this way?

Finally, and as discussed, while management will do much of the legwork in choosing an auditor, it is the board that ultimately engages the firm. One of the earliest steps in the audit process is that the audit firm will typically provide your board with a planning document listing the audit firm's responsibilities, management's responsibilities, and the responsibilities of the board members themselves. Board members can review the planning document to identify any potential risk areas within the organization. For example, the board may not be comfortable with the way your organization has been approving expenses before they are paid and may ask the auditor to evaluate your organization's internal controls around its expense approval process.

Know what to expect from the audit process

Once your board has selected an auditor, an engagement letter will need to be prepared by the audit firm and signed by the parties.

The first year working with a new auditing firm will typically involve the heaviest lifting in terms of workload for the organization. In addition to reviewing all the organization's financials, the auditor will request and check your articles/certificate of incorporation (or state equivalent), your IRS determination letter recognizing 501(c)(3) status, and various other governance documents and background details, which it will not need to request in subsequent years unless those documents have changed. To keep both parties organized, the auditor will likely use a file management system, so that you and your team can upload the relevant documents upon request.

Once you and your team have provided answers to the auditor's initial list of requests, after reviewing that information, the auditor will undoubtedly have follow-up questions and requests for your team to respond to. Additionally, the auditor will request confirmation of bank balances and the amounts of any large grants the organization has received (which they will cross-check directly with the third parties). The auditor will also want opinions from any lawyers who were paid during the year to ensure that the organization has no contingent liabilities that haven't been recorded.

If, during the audit, the auditor encounters issues, which could range from shortcomings with internal controls to a lack of cooperation with management to an excess of journal entries needing to be adjusted, the auditor will issue a management letter to the board detailing these.

In the wrap-up phase, the auditor will send a draft of the audit to management for their review and sign-off. Before the auditor issues the final audit, management will be required to provide the auditor with a signed management representation letter, which is a letter from management to the auditor confirming that the financial statements are accurate and complete and that all relevant information has been disclosed during the audit. When presenting the final version of the audit, the auditor will also review the audit and the audit process with the board and answer any questions the board may have. During this meeting, the auditor might also review with the board any new accounting pronouncements that could affect the organization in the future. The last step is for the board to vote to approve the audit.

Transparency is essential, and it is management's responsibility to ensure that a direct line of communication is established between the auditor and the board. Doing so provides the board with confidence that they are getting the straight scoop and that the auditor's commentary and feedback are not being "filtered" in any way by management.

Keep in mind that it is management's responsibility, not the auditor's, to prepare and present the organization's financial statements accurately. An audit is largely an opinion on those statements.

Note also that CPA standards require auditors to conduct an audit with professional skepticism. This means that, in conducting the audit, the auditor maintains a questioning mindset, critically assesses audit evidence, and remains alert to possible misstatements due to error or fraud rather than simply accepting information at face value.

Anticipate common audit challenges

As we have discussed, an audit should highlight any financial deficiencies within an organization, such as a lack of internal controls or a poor grants management system.

An audit will quickly reveal whether your financial team has consistently done the day-to-day work throughout the year or scrambled to do everything at the last minute in preparation for the audit. If the auditor sees a flood of journal entries for payroll reconciliations as of December 31 (if that is when your fiscal year ends), they will question why none of this work was done during the year and how much more accurate the financials would have been if the organization had released them as of March 31, for example. Ultimately, this raises the question: Can your organization produce accurate financials throughout the year? If the auditor finds that the organization cannot consistently produce accurate and timely financial statements throughout the year, it may interpret this as a material weakness. Addressing those issues proactively not only improves your systems but also reassures funders and the board that you are committed to continuous improvement.

"Leading organizations strengthen their controls by performing monthly closings rather than waiting until year-end to reconcile accounts. By recording prepaids, depreciation, and other adjustments systematically throughout the year, they establish more accurate financial reporting and reduce reliance on estimates at year-end."

Gus Saliba

Throughout the audit, the auditor will check the accounting activities recorded during the year against the organization's policies and procedures manual. If you don't already have a policies and procedures manual, one should be drafted immediately, formally adopted by your board, and documented in the meeting minutes. If your organization does have a policies and procedures manual in place, the auditor will reference it to ensure that accounting activities throughout the year were performed in a manner consistent with the manual. For example, the auditor will review how you record cash receipts and disbursements, how capital expenditures have been expensed or capitalized based on the threshold for capitalizing fixed assets, whether two signatures are required for checks over a certain amount, and at what point the CEO must approve bills.

When it comes to grants management, your auditor will want to know whether each of your grants is restricted or unrestricted, conditional or unconditional, at what point they are released from any restrictions, and how expenses are applied toward your grants. They will require any adjustments or deviations from the original grant agreement to be in writing and signed by both parties.

Finally, your auditor will want to know that your grants management system is properly integrated with your accounting software. If you are managing your grants in a separate Excel spreadsheet but failing to record the associated revenue, spending, and fund restrictions in your accounting system, your auditor will view that as a major internal control weakness.

Respond effectively

If your organization receives feedback, either informally or formally, from your auditor, it is important that your organization makes the necessary adjustments so that those issues don't persist and are rectified in subsequent years. Depending on the severity and extent of the auditor's comments, your response may range from implementing a technology solution to changing the way workflow and approvals are structured to making personnel changes. Thoughtful, timely action on audit findings is a hallmark of a healthy organization, not a sign of failure.

There are three types of deficiencies that auditors can report: a recommendation; a significant deficiency, which indicates that a more serious situation exists; and a material weakness, which is the most concerning of the three.

Failing to address items identified by your auditors year in and year out sends a very negative message to your funders and stakeholders. For funders to continue to support your organization, not only must your organization execute its mission, but you must also produce accurate, transparent, and compliant financial information. High on funders' lists of reasons not to continue to fund an organization is receiving a copy of an auditor's management letter highlighting deficiencies that you have neglected to fix. Your board, too, will grow impatient if deficiencies raised by the auditor are not resolved swiftly.

Summary

- **Form 990 must be prepared carefully and thoroughly each year:** Form 990 is a public-facing compliance document that goes beyond financials and discloses information regarding leadership, governance, and operations, which is critical for transparency and donor trust.

- **Preparation should happen year-round:** Working early with a qualified nonprofit tax preparer, rather than preparing your financials after the fiscal year ends, helps ensure accuracy and reduces stress.

- **Anticipate IRS scrutiny:** The IRS scrutinizes filings for red flags, such as excessive compensation, UBI, or poor allocation of funds. Strong documentation and internal review processes will help you avoid penalties and protect your organization's exempt status.

- **The value of an audit goes beyond compliance:** Even when not legally required, audits can enhance credibility with funders, confirm internal financial accuracy, and serve as a strategic tool to elevate an organization's stature and transparency.

- **Preparation and timing are essential:** Conducting a successful audit requires early planning and a strong, collaborative relationship with auditors, especially from management and the board.

- **Audit findings must be promptly addressed:** Whether feedback highlights minor issues or material weaknesses, it is crucial to act on auditor recommendations promptly to maintain funder trust and improve your financial processes over time.

EIGHT

Mission: Accomplished

Finance is one of the most misunderstood and underprioritized functions in the nonprofit world, particularly among leaders who entered this work out of passion, purpose, and a desire to change the world. For many nonprofit founders and CEOs, the mission comes first, always. You are in the field delivering programs, engaging the community, and driving outcomes. The back office? That has always felt like someone else's job. You did not sign up for forecasting cash flow, performing reconciliations, or parsing Form 990. So, you hire others to take it on.

But what if they aren't doing it well? How would you know until it's too late?

That question is the heartbeat of this book, and the reason I created the *IMPACT Framework for Nonprofits™*. Designed for executive directors and nonprofit CEOs, IMPACT offers a strategic and practical roadmap to help you lead your organization with financial integrity, confidence, and clarity so you can achieve your mission *without compromising your ambition.*

From crisis to competence

As we saw in the opening chapter, the cost of financial mismanagement is steep. Whether caused by under-qualified finance staff, ineffective internal controls, or reactive oversight, many nonprofits face crises that threaten their mission. Auditors may lose confidence in working with your organization. Funders may lose trust. Ultimately, the IRS may question your exempt status. These aren't hypothetical risks; they are very real dangers, and they are more common than most organizations realize.

While the roots of these problems often stem from an increase in programs, grants, and staff, the solution isn't to pull back. It is to build forward with financial systems that scale with your mission.

IMPACT exists to help you do exactly that.

Internal controls are non-negotiable

A strong financial foundation begins with internal controls – safeguarding cash and assets, defining roles clearly, and building structured processes to reduce the risk of fraud or error. These controls don't require a large budget, but they do require intentional design. Tools such as segregation of duties, approval thresholds, and vendor verification protocols can all be implemented with lean teams and tight resources, especially with the help of automation or outsourced services.

But policies are only half the equation. Culture matters just as much. A "zero tolerance" stance toward breaches, paired with a transparent, whistleblower-friendly environment, reinforces accountability at every level. This, in turn, builds trust with your board, funders, auditors, and community.

Grant management is a team sport

For many nonprofits, grants are the lifeblood of their funding model, and grant compliance is often where things break down. Development teams chase opportunities, program staff deliver outcomes, and finance is often left to clean up the reporting. If these teams aren't in lockstep, you risk breaking donor agreements, misreporting expenses, or even having to return funds.

That is why grants must be managed collaboratively, with finance at the table from the start. Strategic communication across departments, accurate tagging of expenses, proactive funder engagement, and monthly reconciliation processes all ensure audit readiness and funding sustainability.

Hope is not a strategy

Too often, leaders "hope" that their financial challenges will resolve themselves. As we have seen, ignoring issues or delaying action only deepens the problem. You need a reliable, repeatable framework that creates predictability and confidence. Regularly assess your financial systems, identify weak points, and implement practical, results-oriented solutions.

With the *IMPACT Framework for Nonprofits*™, you now have a guide to help you build financial systems that support, rather than distract from, your mission and ensure that what *needs* to be done *actually* gets done.

Transparency builds trust

Financial transparency isn't just about numbers. It is about making your internal financial health visible and understandable to all stakeholders, especially those without a finance background. Board members, staff, and funders should all feel confident in your reporting, processes, and financial direction.

To achieve the level of transparency your stakeholders expect, establish regular financial reporting rhythms, deliver financial data in digestible formats, and maintain clear protocols for what gets reported and when. The *IMPACT Framework for Nonprofits*™ prioritizes transparency, helping you instill organizational trust through consistent and clear communication.

Conservative planning creates stability

Nonprofit finance can be unforgiving when things go wrong. When revenue arrives late or expenses go over budget, there is little room for error unless you have planned carefully and are well prepared. As a result, take a conservative approach to budgeting and forecasting by underestimating income, overestimating expenses, and always maintaining a margin of safety.

Liquidity is the backbone of financial stability. In practice, aim for at least ninety days of cash on hand if you have regular, predictable funding streams, and at least 180 days if your operations are grant-dependent or reliant on donations. Reserves are not a luxury; they are a necessity. Without them, the risks multiply, and one missed payroll or unpaid invoice can turn into an existential crisis.

Be precise—the details drive the mission

As a nonprofit leader, your vision is expansive, and you are focused on outcomes, community, and long-term impact. But in finance, precision is power. Execution lives in the details: reconciliations, tagging, timing, and approvals. These aren't just administrative tasks; they are the disciplines that make your big-picture goals achievable.

That is why healthy skepticism and sharp attention to detail are essential. If something does not make sense, dig in. Get curious. Ask questions. Your role isn't to have all the answers; it is to ensure that your finance team delivers the right ones, clearly, consistently, and on time.

I developed the *IMPACT Framework for Nonprofits™* over many years of working with organizations whose financial systems were broken, unclear, or entirely absent. The framework is designed to provide a strategic, actionable roadmap for addressing the recurring challenges nonprofits face so that your finance function becomes a source of confidence rather than confusion.

When implemented thoughtfully, IMPACT allows you to build a best-in-class finance function within your organization that not only ensures compliance and financial clarity but also unlocks alignment and momentum across your leadership team. It gives you the structure to lead confidently and the peace of mind to stay focused on the mission that brought you here in the first place. In the end, financial leadership is not separate from mission; it is what protects it. When your systems are strong, your reporting is clear, and your team is aligned, you unlock the full power of your organization. That is the promise of IMPACT: a stronger organization, a protected mission, and a leader fully equipped to move it all forward.

Acknowledgments

I am deeply grateful to the many nonprofit leaders and colleagues whose voices and insights helped shape this book. To those whose stories and perspectives I have quoted, thank you for your generosity in sharing your experience so that others may learn from it. To that end, I would like to thank Aaron Fox, Ana Morgado, Charlie Haraway, Gus Saliba, and Robert Price.

To my beta readers, including Aaron Fox, Catherine Holland, Elizabeth Green, and Gideon Stein, your thoughtful feedback pushed me to clarify, refine, and strengthen the ideas in these pages. This book is sharper and more useful because of your engagement and care.

A special acknowledgment goes to Gideon Stein, my collaborator and friend across a lifetime of work. Your wisdom, counsel, and belief in me have been constant anchors, and I could not imagine my professional journey without you.

I also want to recognize Ana Morgado, with whom I have had the privilege of collaborating closely for nearly twenty years. You have been an extraordinary partner in so much of the work I do, bringing commitment, creativity, and insight that have elevated every project we've shared.

Finally, to my wife and children, who gave me patience, encouragement, and love throughout the long process of writing. Your support made this project possible in every way.

The Author

Ryan Alexander is the founder of RA Partners, a firm that supports nonprofit leaders in building and strengthening their financial strategy, infrastructure, and capacity to advance their missions. Drawing on more than two decades of experience across finance, operations, and social impact, he created the *IMPACT Framework for Nonprofits*™, a practical model for building best-in-class finance functions that drive organizational effectiveness and accountability.

Ryan has served as a senior executive at two software companies and as chief financial officer of a rapidly growing education organization, where he helped scale operations from $40 million to $140 million in three years. Earlier in his career, he grew a facilities investment fund from inception into a $300 million program financing high-performing schools nationwide.

He has worked with public charities and private foundations across the country to transform complex and often suboptimal financial operations into cohesive, transparent systems, earning a reputation for transforming complexity into clarity for nonprofit leaders.

Ryan lives in New York City with his wife and children.

⊕ ra.partners

www.ingramcontent.com/pod-product-compliance
Lightning Source LLC
Chambersburg PA
CBHW042120190326
41519CB00031B/7562